Money
and the Way *of*
Wisdom

Insights from the Book of Proverbs

Timothy J. Sandoval, PhD

Walking Together, Finding the Way ®
SKYLIGHT PATHS®
PUBLISHING
Woodstock, Vermont

Money and the Way of Wisdom:
Insights from the Book of Proverbs

2008 Quality Paperback Edition, First Printing
© 2008 by Timothy J. Sandoval

For information regarding permission to reprint material from this book, please mail or fax your request in writing to SkyLight Paths Publishing, Permissions Department, at the address / fax number listed below, or e-mail your request to permissions@skylightpaths.com.

Grateful acknowledgment is given for permission to use the photo from Bildarchiv Preussischer Kulturbesitz/Art Resource, NY.

Library of Congress Cataloging-in-Publication Data
Sandoval, Timothy J.
Money and the way of wisdom: insights from the book of Proverbs / Timothy J. Sandoval.
p. cm.
Includes bibliographical references.
ISBN-13: 978-1-59473-245-4 (pbk.)
ISBN-10: 1-59473-245-0 (pbk.)
1. Bible. O.T. Proverbs—Criticism, interpretation, etc. 2. Wealth—Biblical teaching.
3. Money—Biblical teaching. I. Title.
BS1465.6.W35S365 2008
241'.64—dc22
2008029750

10 9 8 7 6 5 4 3 2 1

Manufactured in the United States of America
Cover Design: Tim Holtz
Cover Photo: ©iStockphoto.com/Christine Balderas
Coin Photo: ©iStockphoto.com/Eli Mordechai

SkyLight Paths Publishing is creating a place where people of different spiritual traditions come together for challenge and inspiration, a place where we can help each other understand the mystery that lies at the heart of our existence.

SkyLight Paths sees both believers and seekers as a community that increasingly transcends traditional boundaries of religion and denomination—people wanting to learn from each other, *walking together, finding the way.*

SkyLight Paths, "Walking Together, Finding the Way" and colophon are trademarks of LongHill Partners, Inc., registered in the U.S. Patent and Trademark Office.

Walking Together, Finding the Way®
Published by SkyLight Paths Publishing
A Division of LongHill Partners, Inc.
Sunset Farm Offices, Route 4, P.O. Box 237
Woodstock, VT 05091
Tel: (802) 457-4000 Fax: (802) 457-4004
www.skylightpaths.com

Para mis suegros, Don Tiburcio y Doña Antonia Yax,
quienes no han sido ricos según este mundo,
pero sí lo han sido en sabiduria.

For my in-laws, Don Tiburcio and Doña Antonia Yax,
who though never wealthy by the world's standards,
are rich in wisdom.

CONTENTS

Introduction

The richest fifth of the world's people
consumes 86 percent of all goods and services
while the poorest fifth consumes just 1.3 percent.
—United Nations Human Development Report of 1998

Capitalism can make a society rich....
Don't ask it to make you happy as well.
—The Economist, vol. 381

The Predicament of Money

Economic inequalities in our world are staggering. More than 50 percent of the global population scrapes through life in poverty, while those of us who live in the richest countries in the world are becoming more and more defined by what our money and prosperity can buy us.[1] We are bombarded with advertisements—on TV, on radio, in magazines, on billboards, on the Internet—encouraging us to use our money to consume more and more: a fancier car, a bigger house, a better stereo, and that new dining room set. When financial markets start to flag, we are encouraged to spend yet *more*, if not for ourselves then for the health of the nation's economy. The implicit promise is that our spending will make for a happy, fulfilled, and meaningful life—a good life in a strong society. As the modern, somewhat cynical proverb goes: "The one who dies with the most toys wins!"

Yet at the same time, for many of us—whatever our spiritual tradition, or none at all—there is a spiritual vacuum, a lack of meaning amid our prosperity, a sense that the promises of a good life that our consumerist culture offers are hollow, undeliverable. Some of us spend more and more hours in the office, forfeiting the joys that time spent with family and friends might bring and hoping that this investment in time, and the higher earnings it provides, will lead to a significant happiness payoff. According to the National Bureau of Economic Research, for instance, the number of college-educated males who regularly work more than fifty hours a week rose from 22 percent in 1980 to 30.5 percent in 2001.[2] Others among us are persistently anxious about our money, even in the midst of the prosperity that our homes, rich and diverse food, good education and health, and abundant possessions provide us. After all, we still have house payments, grocery bills, the kids' university tuition, that high-deductible health plan premium, and the new car payments that never seem to end. Plus, we want to continue financially supporting our church, synagogue, or other spiritual home, as well as organizations that are doing such good work downtown or around the globe. In the midst of it all, we may wonder, "Will we ever 'arrive'?"

Exacerbating the feelings of hollowness and anxiety that some of us feel—even as we continue to chase happiness via our pocketbooks—is the genuine need we see around us every day, from the homeless vet looking for change on the off-ramp or the migrant laborer struggling clandestinely in a strange land, to the unfathomable reports of famine and global poverty we hear on the evening news. We know we should help—and we will (or we will help more), just as soon as we help ourselves a little more, just as soon as our money and prosperity finally secure our own well-being, our own happiness.

We all have heard that money can't buy us happiness. But why should any of us dwell on this point, especially those of us who are relatively well off? Money may not be able to buy us happiness, but it can buy a lot that seems to make our lives pretty good.

For one thing, sages across the centuries have long recognized that material prosperity does not inevitably result in spiritual fulfillment and that continued, anxious attempts to buy "salvation" (as it were) actually diminish human well-being. Our pursuit of the "good life" through the frenzied pursuit of wealth not only may not pay off, it actually carries its own costs. Even "nonsages" have begun to recognize that the unbridled pursuit of wealth and money can produce the sort of anxiety and diminished quality of relations with family and friends that we noted above; it can also contribute to things like mental illness. A report by James Montier of the investment bank Dresdner Kleinwort Wasserstein, for instance, suggests that "paranoia, narcissism and attention deficit disorders are just some of the afflictions more likely to dog you if you pursue purely materialistic goals."[3]

Large-scale, unbridled quests for money and riches, moreover, can also produce great economic inequalities like those we see in our world today. Significant economic inequality, in turn, can contribute to a range of social problems and generate strife between members of the same community, society, or country. In the rapidly changing nation of China, for example, a 2007 poll by the *China Youth Daily* found that 57 percent of those questioned were unhappy with the "rich" and used terms such as *extravagant, greedy,* and *corrupt* to describe them. A huge majority, 93 percent, also thought the rich should be "socially responsible." Yet the same percentage of people wanted to be rich, too.[4] Despite a rough but clear sense of the moral dangers that the pursuit and attainment of significant wealth entails (people associate greed and corruption with the rich), most people who responded to this poll nonetheless desired to be rich, believing, one assumes, that wealth somehow holds the key to a good and flourishing life.

Yet the inequalities and class tensions that arise from the pursuit of wealth, as well as the belief that money equals happiness, are not limited to far-off places like China. In the United States and other affluent countries in the West, poor and working-class discontent with the excessive rewards of Wall Street hedge fund managers and executives' "golden parachutes" is easy to discern. And although national incomes in these countries have increased significantly over the last several decades, the percentage of people who describe themselves as happy has remained constant.[5] As Jennifer Michael Hecht, author of *The Happiness Myth,* has stated, "Above the poverty line, money is not the answer to happiness."[6]

Our Response to the Predicament of Money

How, then, ought those of us—whether middle class or people of means—who possess some wealth, but may lack the full, meaningful life we desire, respond to this situation? Some of us, no doubt, have simply decided to live with, or ignore, the tension and anxiety that our money, and our pursuit of money, creates in our lives. Although experience tells us that prosperity does not hold the key to a genuinely good life, somewhere deep inside, a good number of us still hope that with a little more time, a few more promotions, or the right investment strategy, we *will* get the happiness payoff we so desperately, sometimes secretly, long for. Ultimately we may agree with John D. Rockefeller, who when asked, "How much money is enough?" supposedly famously quipped, "One dollar more."

Others among us, however, seek to move beyond the tension and anxiety. We look to whatever spiritual resource we can find for some sort of enlightenment, some way out of the predicament. Some of us look to simplify our lives, or we seek peace of mind by supporting charities and joining the efforts of causes and organizations working for a more just world. Some of us turn to meditation to calm our troubled and anxious spirits. Others mine the texts and interpretations of Buddhism, Hinduism, or the world's indigenous peoples for answers, hoping that among the insights of these disparate faiths and cultures we will find some wisdom for living in our world today. We buy whatever spiritual advice book we can get our hands on—maybe even this one. We are consumers, after all.

The Bible and the Book of Proverbs

This book is about helping you break out of the predicament, whatever spiritual path you follow. But it's different, too. It's not a self-help book, though it talks about the ways some of us might change how we think about, and what we do with, our money—for example, whether our investments ought to be made in a socially conscious way. But, more important, it asks us both to delve beneath the surface of our individual behaviors and to examine our fundamental moral orientations in order to discover whether our actions and beliefs are beneficial to our spirit and our world. Giving to charity may be a good thing to do—but why, and what are the limitations of such good work? Through this book we can begin to ask the deeper questions of ourselves; in the process, we can discover what our fundamental priorities are for *all* the ways we deal with our wealth, however much we may possess.

Like many other books, this one looks to the wisdom of people from a time and place very different from our own to help us find our way when it comes to our money and the way we should, and should not, deal with it. Yet the tradition that this book turns to for guidance—the Bible and, especially, the Book of Proverbs—is a touchstone for many people, especially Jews and Christians, and may be a bit more familiar than other spiritual sources.

The Bible is sacred scripture for many. For others, it is an interesting historical document or cultural artifact. Still others may view it as a key tool in religion's efforts to unduly control and oppress human beings. Over the course of my many years of studying and teaching the Bible in academic and religious environments—in churches, university classrooms, and theological schools—I have witnessed how those who seriously engage the biblical texts, even skeptics and nonreligious students, consistently find much to ponder in the "Book of Books." Indeed, even if certain biblical perspectives—for example the role of women in religious communities and society—are not and cannot be adopted by many modern readers of the Bible, those who read the scripture critically but also with an openness to learning are rarely disappointed with the effort. Serious study and reflection on the Bible nearly always leads us to discover new and valuable insights into many of the issues and concerns that we face in our lives and in the contemporary world.

Discovering the Way of Wisdom

More than any other book of the Bible, the biblical Book of Proverbs discusses one of these topics of broad contemporary concern— money and questions of wealth and poverty, the rich and the poor. Although Proverbs is often thought to be nothing more than a simple and straightforward guide to worldly success, including financial success, closer examination shows that the book's pithy sayings and elegant poems form a sophisticated and clever system of rhetoric that transcends the comparatively superficial "advice" it appears to give. Instead, it plumbs profound truths about a host of matters we are still concerned with today. The ancient sages who composed and edited the book wanted to convince their original audience, and subsequently those of us who read the book today, to acquire "wisdom," or those values and virtues or character traits that can help us lead not merely financially prosperous lives but, more fundamentally, the fulfilled and morally upstanding lives so many of us long for. According to Proverbs, the moral teachings this book holds out to us are of even greater worth than material wealth and should be the primary objects of our search for happiness. For if we have wisdom, we have the key to other blessings, such as peace of mind and a sense of security, harmonious personal and social relations, and a healthy relationship with money. These are the benefits of the *way of wisdom* that the sages of Proverbs invite us to choose, the characteristics of which we will explore. To reject this path, according to the Book of Proverbs, is to follow the *way of folly.*

A Modern Sage and the Sages of Proverbs

Dr. Martin Luther King Jr. once famously asserted that "the arc of the moral universe is long, but it bends toward justice."[7] In a very real way, Dr. King's claim is analogous to the kind of claims the sages of Proverbs make throughout the Book of Proverbs when they, almost naively to modern ears, confidently assume that all will end well for the wise and righteous, but that the foolish and wicked will come to naught. It would be an easy exercise to review the history of any nation or people and their relations to one another and discover a string of wars of aggression, maltreatment of the poor, corruption of legal systems, genocides, and violence in the name of gods and religions—all things that would seem to disprove Dr. King's claim. Indeed, the *Maafa,* or destruction of African peoples in the transatlantic slave trade and beyond; or the *Shoah* (the Jewish Holocaust) carried out by the German Nazis in the 1930s and 1940s; or the fact that 50 percent of the world continues to live on $2 a day or less are enough to make us believe that Dr. King was just plain wrong.[8] If the real history of human interaction is any guide, we might assert with some justification that rather than the moral arc of the cosmos bending toward justice, it bends toward injustice, violence, destruction, and suffering.

However, this would be to misunderstand Dr. King's words. Dr. King was not, in my view, offering a kind of statement that might be verified empirically. He was not primarily asking us to look around and see in the great historical events of human history, and in our own day, scientific proof of the arc of the moral universe bending toward justice. As Dr. King said, this arc is "long." Like a desert highway that stretches to the horizon, we cannot see from our present position whence it originates, where it ends, the twists and turns it might take beyond the horizon, or even the literal curve it traces over the face of the earth right beneath our feet. Rather, Dr. King's statement is an assertion of faith regarding the real or true structure of the cosmos. Dr. King was convinced that "There is a creative force in this universe, working to pull down the gigantic mountains of evil," such as racism and poverty.[9] He was convinced that the genuine shape of the cosmos is one that ultimately favors justice.

Yet if Dr. King's claim that the arc of the moral cosmos bends toward justice is not the sort of claim that can be empirically verified, what sort of claim is it? What was he attempting to do in uttering such powerful words? I contend that Dr. King's claim might be understood as doing at least two important things. First, it was the kind of claim that, if accepted, if believed to be true, would serve as a solid foundation for moral or ethical action in the world. From the civil rights movement of the 1950s and 1960s through to our own time, those who have accepted Dr. King's claim have believed themselves to be standing on the correct or right side of the moral cosmos. They have understood their lives and actions to be in accordance with the true nature of the universe. And an understanding of one's life and one's actions in this way is not necessarily something that can be dismissed lightly as mere "pie in the sky" hope or simplistic faith. Rather, it powerfully grounds our motivation for ethical action in the world. The earnest belief that Dr. King and others held (and many still hold), that the arc of the moral universe does indeed bend toward justice, constructed a powerful underpinning for working for racial justice in the face of fire hoses, police dogs, lynchings, mob violence, and legal, institutionalized racism. To boldly face such real-life resistance to justice requires a deep confidence that your way is, despite evidence to the contrary, the right way.

Dr. King's assertion also served a second function, as an invitation for all people to get themselves on the right side of the moral cosmos, to align their beings, their actions, and their communities with the genuine structure of reality, with the true shape of the universe, which "bends toward justice."

When, as we shall see, the sages of Proverbs claim that good things will come to the wise and righteous, and that the wicked and foolish should expect that their way will end badly, they are not offering us literal statements about their observations of the world. Rather, they are using poetic language to make a claim similar to Dr. King's. They are claiming that wisdom is at the heart of the cosmos and that the invitation to follow wisdom's way, to live up to the values and virtues that the sages articulate, including those about money and social justice, is an invitation to align one's life with the genuine structure of the cosmos. Indeed, in Proverbs 8 the sages claim explicitly that "The Lord," the Divine, "created" (or acquired) wisdom "at the beginning" of God's creation or "work" (8:22). Wisdom, Proverbs says, was with the Divine, "before the mountains had been shaped" (8:25) and before God had "made earth and fields" or "established the heavens" (8:26–27). Wisdom, moreover, at the moment of creation, acted with God "like a master worker," "rejoicing" (8:30) in the world and in the humans whom God created (8:31).

> ^{22}The LORD created me at the beginning of his work, the
> first of his acts of long ago.
> ^{23}Ages ago I was set up, at the first, before the beginning of
> the earth.
> ^{24}When there were no depths I was brought forth, when
> there were no springs abounding with water.
> ^{25}Before the mountains had been shaped, before the hills, I
> was brought forth—
> ^{26}when he had not yet made earth and fields, or the world's
> first bits of soil.
> ^{27}When he established the heavens, I was there, when he
> drew a circle on the face of the deep,
> ^{28}when he made firm the skies above, when he established
> the fountains of the deep,
> ^{29}when he assigned to the sea its limit, so that the waters
> might not transgress his command, when he marked out
> the foundations of the earth,
> ^{30}then I was beside him, like a master worker; and I was
> daily his delight, rejoicing before him always,
> ^{31}rejoicing in his inhabited world and delighting in the
> human race. (Proverbs 8:22–31; NRSV)

According to the sages in Proverbs 8, wisdom is thus "built into" the very fabric of the cosmos from the beginning of creation.

Although the sages of Proverbs speak to us from a distant time and place, they bid all of us who read their book and who are open to instruction in their ancient wisdom to "get on the right side of things." Whether we are old or young, female or male, poor or, yes, even wealthy, we are called by the sages of old to align ourselves with the way of wisdom, which is also what gives shape to the cosmos. (It's worth making a distinction here between wealth and the sages' use of the term *rich*. In the eyes of the sages, possessing wealth would inevitably put someone in a certain precarious position, morally speaking. This, however, was not the same thing as displaying self-centeredness and other negative characteristics associated with a particular class of wealthy people called the "rich.")

Yet how might we begin to accept the invitation of Proverbs today? How might we start to respond to this book's wisdom about money and riches that comes to us from so far away and so long ago? How might those of us who are privileged to possess great wealth (especially when compared with so many others in the world) begin to align our lives with the moral vision of a book that, as we shall see, so often characterizes the "rich" as greedy, harsh, and lacking faith? These are some of the questions we will be considering and attempting to answer as we explore what Proverbs has to say about money and the way of wisdom and how wisdom might help us craft a vision for the relationship with money we have in our own lives.

Accessing Proverbs' Wisdom—The Path Ahead

Before we make our way fully into Proverbs' clever system of rhetoric and its wisdom about money, we first need to know a few other things about both proverbs generally and the Book of Proverbs specifically. Thus, before turning to a close study of the many poems and sayings in Proverbs that speak of wealth and poverty, in chapter 1 we will explore the phenomena of proverbs in general and the ways that the proverbs found in the Book of Proverbs are similar to, and different from, other types of proverbs. This foundational understanding about the kinds of proverbs many of us know and use every day (as well as the kinds of proverbs we find in the Book of

Proverbs) will help us uncover the particular insights about money and riches that Proverbs holds for us today.

Chapter 2 lays additional important groundwork for our study of money and wisdom in Proverbs by answering fundamental questions about the Book of Proverbs itself, such as when and where it was written, by whom, and how it was put together. This chapter also focuses on the larger literary context in which the individual proverbs of the book are embedded. Recognizing this literary context will help us see the rich possibilities for understanding Proverbs' often-overlooked teachings about wealth and poverty. We will especially consider how the very first lines of Proverbs, its Prologue, provide a crucial interpretive key to understanding the book and how the long sophisticated poems that comprise the first nine chapters of Proverbs use the language of wealth to highlight the preeminent value of wisdom's way. We will see how, taken together, the Prologue and the long wisdom poems in Proverbs 1–9 redefine what we consider of value, and teach us to look beyond the literal, surface meaning of the text to reveal the depth of Proverbs' riches.

The subsequent chapters in Proverbs then turn to the dozens and dozens of short, artful sayings (what we usually think of as proverbs) that speak of money, wealth, and the rich and the poor, such as "What good is money in the hand of a fool to purchase wisdom, when he has no mind?" (Proverbs 17:16; cf. JPS). Chapter 3 initially focuses on how some of these short sayings highlight the worth of wisdom's way, similar to the poems of Proverbs 1–9. This chapter also examines other proverbs that highlight particular virtues, such as diligence and the worth of hard work, which the ancient sages valued highly and which can also be valuable for those of us today who seek to walk in wisdom's way.

Chapter 4 narrows the focus somewhat by considering those proverbs in the Book of Proverbs that offer us concrete instruction for living with our money, such as how we ought to conduct ourselves in the marketplace and what our relationship to those who are economically less fortunate ought to be. "Those who are generous are blessed, for they share their bread with the poor" (Proverbs 22:9). This chapter also highlights the sayings that reveal the ancient sages' multifaceted view of social justice and the important role that social justice plays in Proverbs' vision of what wisdom entails.

Chapter 5 then examines a special category of proverbs that, at first glance, appear to make neutral observations about wealth and poverty and the rich and the poor, noting, for instance, the advantage people of means sometimes enjoy over those with less, such as Proverbs 22:7, which tell us that "The rich person rules over the poor and the borrower is a slave to the lender...." However, as we will see, these proverbs function as critiques of the rich and excessive wealth. Chapter 5 also studies the very last verses of Proverbs that constitute the poem to the so-called woman of worth. This figure embodies significant aspects of the book's teaching, including its teaching about money and justice, and thus should be regarded, at least in part, as a symbolic representation of wisdom and wisdom's virtues.

Throughout our entire exploration of money and the way of wisdom, I will offer some thoughts about, and examples of, how we might begin to "translate" the ancient wisdom of Proverbs for our own day and time. Recalling Dr. King's powerful image of the arc of the moral universe, I will attempt to sketch trajectories of thought from the sages' time and place to our own so that we might better know how wisdom, and not money, could lead to a secure, spiritually fulfilled, and happy life—a life characterized not by anxiety and tension or by isolation and strife in our relations and communities, but by the genuine well-being that just social relations bring and the peace of mind that comes through recognizing and pursuing that which possesses true value in human life.

A Note on Translation

Unless otherwise noted, the translations of biblical verses in this book are my own. Arguments for particular translation choices can be found in *The Discourse of Wealth and Poverty in the Book of Proverbs*.[10] On many occasions, my renderings of particular proverbs rely on, or adopt, the translations of the New Revised Standard Version (NRSV)[11] or the Jewish Publication Society (JPS)[12]. I have also, on occasion, referenced the New International Version (NIV).[13] Whenever I explicitly adopt the translation of one of these versions, I note the version. When my rendering of the biblical text is influenced by, but not entirely identical with one of the above versions, I invite the reader to compare my translation with that version (e.g., "cf. NRSV"). The index on pp. 165–166 provides page numbers for all of the verses translated or quoted throughout the text.

CHAPTER 1

"Proverbs" and the "Book" of Proverbs

¡En boca cerrada no entran moscas!

"In a closed mouth, flies don't enter!" my father would sometimes say, in Spanish. It is one of the few Spanish phrases that my Mexican-American father, who otherwise wanted his children to speak English, used to say to my three siblings and me—usually when he wanted us to stop bickering around the dinner table. What events would have precipitated Dad's pronouncement? Perhaps an argument over whose turn it was to take out the garbage. In our house, those sorts of arguments would escalate rapidly among my brother, sisters, and me—"It's your turn!" "No, it's your turn!"—until my father would intervene and say loudly and sternly, but without shouting, "As Grandpa Sandoval used to say, '*¡En boca cerrada no entran moscas!*'" This quickly put an end to our argument, lest we risk an even sterner rebuke. We knew what he meant, but we also knew what he *meant*.

Dad didn't use many proverbs—in fact, I can't recall any others that he used regularly—but the one he did use is one that my siblings and I still remember. Maybe you can conjure up the memory of someone in your life—a parent or grandparent, that woman who lived around the corner, an elder in church or synagogue—who

1

would regularly talk to you, instruct you, rebuke you, or command you, using the pithy and colorful language of proverbs:

"An apple a day keeps the doctor away"
   to remind you to eat well and attend to your diet and
   health.

"If you play with matches, you're gonna get burned"
   to warn you away from a potentially harmful
   relationship.

"Early to bed and early to rise makes a man healthy,
   wealthy, and wise"
   to encourage you to live diligently and purposefully.

Proverbs have played some sort of role in each of our lives, and we may be so familiar with a handful of them that we simply take them for granted. But just what is a proverb? Who writes them? How do they actually function in the world—that is, how do they *work* to transmit their wisdom to us? Finding answers to these fundamental questions will help us understand the unique characteristics of proverbs in general and specifically how the proverbs found in the Book of Proverbs can help us to understand that biblical book's wisdom on wealth.

What Is a Proverb?

Every culture has its own stock of proverbs, and many of us know, or remember, someone particularly adept at using proverbs in the different situations in which we find ourselves from day to day. Even so, we may be hard-pressed to identify specifically what makes a proverb a proverb. Yet there are some distinguishing characteristics they all share.

Consider this sentence: "Every article that coruscates is not fashioned from aureate metal." It's a complete, grammatically correct sentence. Some words, like *article, fashioned,* and *metal,* are familiar, but otherwise the sentence feels like a bit of industrial prose. When you first read the sentence, you may not be sure what it means and you may have to look up in a dictionary at least a couple of the words, terms like *coruscate* and *aureate.* It turns out that *coruscate* means "to give forth light" or "to sparkle," and *aureate* is an adjective that means something is "gilded" or of a "golden color."

Thus, with a little dictionary work you can begin to get a handle on the sentence by substituting some of the unfamiliar terms with better-known words so that you end up with something like, "Every article that 'gives forth light' or 'sparkles' is not fashioned from 'gilded' metal (or metal of a 'golden color')." You now have a little better sense of what the sentence means. But this is still a far cry from "All that glitters is not gold"![1]

The difference between the two statements, which in a certain technical sense say the same thing, is stark. The first sentence—"Every article that coruscates is not fashioned from aureate metal"—is long and reveals a somewhat complex syntax or sentence structure. For example, it makes use of a relative clause introduced by *that* and a prepositional phrase that begins with *from.* The words it uses are also not very common or colorful, but rather technical and dull. By contrast, the second sentence—"All that glitters is not gold"—is significantly shorter. It uses only six words as opposed to the ten used in the first sentence. It abbreviates, for instance, "Every article that" to "All that." Its sentence structure is also more straightforward, and it employs common terms like *gold* instead of *aureate metal,* and uses evocative language: *glitters* instead of *coruscates.* Moreover, the first may convey a certain piece of information, but it doesn't *tell* us anything, at least not in the way we understand that the second tells us something of value, something that we can use.

We can thus see that a proverb, in contrast to a more prosaic sentence, is *a short, pithy saying*. But this is only part of the story. As most of us probably realize from the way our grandparents or others made use of proverbs, these short, pithy sayings also regularly carry or present to us *general truths* or a *moral lesson*. They offer us bits of wisdom. Sometimes these lessons may seem self-evident, but often they contain more gravitas than meets the eye. They are sometimes windows into a complex ethical system.

The moral landscape of any society is extraordinarily complex. Hence, subtle distinctions in the range of values and virtues you might discover in the proverbs of any culture are to be expected. Indeed, when citing different proverbs, certain members of a society might be seeking to promote certain kinds of values, while other members may seek to promote different sorts of values with the words and sayings they use. The range of proverbs current in any culture might thus reveal competing values that reflect a social struggle over the moral identity of that society.[2]

Imagine, for example, that you come upon an investment opportunity that is risky, but nonetheless looks promising. Normally a cautious investor, you decide to call two friends for advice. The first, who is even more cautious than you are, says, "Well, that's a tough one, but given the risks, I would say, 'A fool and his money are easily parted!'" You hang up and call your second friend who, by contrast, advises you to remember that "Fortune favors the bold!"

Obviously, in this imaginary situation your two friends are giving you contrary advice about how to proceed. Your first friend uses her proverb to encourage you not to make the risky investment. The second friend deploys a different proverb to counsel you to take that risk.

Note, however, that there is something else at work here besides the particular advice you are gleaning from your friends' words:

Each of the proverbs that the two friends quote carry a particular value or promote a particular kind of virtue *in general*. "A fool and his money are easily parted!" promotes the virtue of cautiousness in financial dealings. By contrast, "Fortune favors the bold!" endorses the virtue of decisiveness.

Because these two proverbs initially appear to be at odds with each other, they may seem to represent two distinct social perspectives. If the two contradictory proverbs are heard often enough within a particular community or social circle, it might mean that people in that community are struggling with one another over whether one or the other value ultimately is, or ought to be, more important in their community or society. We will come back to this observation about how proverbs work when we turn our attention to the array of biblical proverbs that deal with wisdom and money, yet often appear to offer conflicting perspectives. Economic questions—questions of money and wealth—are often highly contested social matters, never more so than today with our increasingly complex financial markets, our debates over the proper role of government regulation, and the increasing stratification of society, with the ever-growing gap between rich and poor.

Yet, as we probe more deeply, we discover that each of the above proverbs, and the values they encourage—cautiousness and resolve, respectively—also are not necessarily opposites or incompatible with each another. One person can hold both these views at the same time. You can be generally cautious, but also able to make bold decisions and not look back. You may well believe in the thriftiness that the adage "A penny saved is a penny earned" connotes, but at other times understand that it is possible to be "penny wise but dollar foolish."

So, too, a larger society can affirm via its proverbs different sorts of values at the same time, proverbs that at first glance may appear contradictory, but form part of a more complicated, nuanced system of moral perspectives. This insight, too, is important to keep in mind when studying the diverse wealth and poverty sayings of Proverbs.

Who Writes and Uses Proverbs?

My father always prefaced his use of *¡En boca cerrada no entran moscas!* with the words, "As Grandpa Sandoval used to say ..." This was not to inform us that Grandpa Sandoval was the actual author of the pithy saying. It wasn't to say that if we went to a book of "Mexican Proverbs" we would find this particular proverb attributed to a certain "Antonio Sandoval, born in Mexico, but residing most recently in Coyote, California." No, what the words "As Grandpa Sandoval used to say" conveyed to us was that my father had learned the proverb—and the value of its wisdom and how and when to use the phrase—from *his* father. The point was not to make a claim about the origins or the authorship of the phrase. It was rather a kind of literary strategy designed to ground the proverb's teaching in a bigger, broader, and older tradition of instruction and authority. Placing the proverb on the lips of a grandfather, an image that in the popular imagination is regularly associated with old age and the insight of long experience, accomplishes precisely that. Even today, when my brother uses the phrase with *his* kids, he says, "as Grandpa Sandoval used to say" not "as *Great*-grandpa Sandoval used to say." I imagine that when my Grandpa Sandoval himself actually used the proverb he also said, "As Grandpa Sandoval used to say ..."

All this is to illustrate a point that folklorists who study the proverbs of different peoples of the world often make: Proverbs generally have no single author in the way that many of us today think about authors penning some original turn of phrase. Rather, proverbs are the product of the collected and collective wisdom of the people of a particular culture or subculture. The wisdom of individual proverbs reflects not merely the insight of a single individual, but the more authoritative wisdom of a broader societal or communal understanding of the way things are, or ought to be, which has been refined over time. Certainly some proverbs are associated with or attributed to a particular person who may have penned some, but not all, of the sayings associated with his name. For instance, we have collections of wise sayings from ancient Egypt that were passed on by scribes with names like Amenemope and Ani. Certain proverbs from ancient Mesopotamia are attributed to wise courtiers like Shuruppak and Ahiqar. The sage Confucius is associated with many of the wise sayings of China. In the United States, wisdom lives on in proverbs like Benjamin Franklin's "Creditors have better memories than debtors," for example.

From ancient civilizations down to modern times, people the world over have used proverbs to make their points, to reinforce their commands, to embellish their language, to support legal cases and offer political advice, and to comment on financial matters.[3] Thanks to the work of folklorists who have recorded and anthologized the proverbial lore from around the globe, we now have easy access to many of these sayings, which carry the wit and wisdom of widely diverse cultures. You can find collections of Mexican proverbs (which would probably include the proverb that my father used to get us kids to pipe down), African-American proverbs, English proverbs, Korean proverbs, Chinese proverbs, Old Irish sayings, as well as the proverbial wisdom of a host of African cultures. In the sixteenth century, the celebrated Flemish painter Pieter Brueghel (1525–1569) recognized the importance of proverbs in the everyday life of the Flemish people and illustrated over one hundred of them. In slightly different form, we still hear some of these sayings relating to money, such as "He throws his money in the water" (He throws his money out the window); or "He can't reach from one loaf of bread to another" (He can't make ends meet).

Because they are a cultural phenomenon more than the result of one individual's observations, proverbs can carry the depth and subtlety of an entire society's received wisdom. It is their remarkable power to effortlessly convey a depth of wisdom that makes them such a popular phenomenon across time and across cultures.

How Do Proverbs Work?

Although every culture has its own stock of proverbs, many of us today—especially in the modern, industrialized, and well-educated West—do not use proverbs in our everyday speech as much as perhaps our grandparents did, or as much as folks from other cultures still do. Why? Partly because proverbs are rooted in spoken, rather than written, language. In societies that have higher literacy rates, where most people read and write well, the use of proverbs (in spoken language) declines.

This is not to say that we no longer use proverbs at all or that no new proverbs are being created. If you scratch beneath the surface of common expressions, you will likely discover quite a few proverbs. For instance, if you have ever responded to someone's floundering attempt to do good by saying, "As they say, 'The road to hell....'" then you have used a portion of a proverb ("The road to hell" being a short form of the proverb "The road to hell is paved with good intentions"). Similarly, if you have ever encouraged a friend to pursue some activity for which he has some talent with the advice "If you got it, flaunt it!" or if you have warned someone about doing a sloppy job on a report with the phrase "Garbage in, garbage out" (a modern-day saying born in the computer age), you have used proverbs.

How we *say* proverbs is important because folklorists who study proverbs and how they work point out that what a proverb

Brueghel, Pieter the Elder (c. 1525-1569). The Netherlandish Proverbs. 1559. Oil on oak panel, 117 x 163 cm. Inv. 1720. Photo: Joerg P. Anders. Gemaeldegalerie, Staatliche Museen zu Berlin, Berlin, Germany. In this sixteenth-century painting, the celebrated Flemish artist illustrated over one hundred proverbs he knew to be current in the Netherlands in his day. Among the more easily recognized sayings depicted by Brueghel are "The big fish eats the little fish," "There's no sense banging your head against a wall," and "All depends on how the cards fall" (the "luck of the draw").

means is determined by its use in a particular *oral* or *speech context*. We grasp the meaning of proverbs by how we utter and hear (not read) them in our everyday lives. But how does this work? According to linguists and rhetoricians, when we hear or make use of a proverb, what we are doing is drawing an analogy, almost intuitively, between the real-life situation in which we find ourselves and the words and images of the spoken proverb.[4]

For example, when my father said, "*¡En boca cerrada no entran moscas!*" to his children who were quarreling around the dinner table, he meant for us to "hush up." Plain and simple. We all knew it. It was clear from the context in which he said it. He had said it before and he would say it again in essentially the same situation. But more subtly and almost unconsciously, we also all knew that a fly buzzing around in our mouths, trying to sneak down our throats, forcing us to grimace and cough and spit, was not pleasant. If we did not want to experience something that was likewise "not pleasant"—such as a further scolding or some punishment—we should make sure our bickering mouths remained closed and silent.

Yet that isn't the only way that my father *could* have "used" that well-known Mexican proverb with my siblings and me. He could have also said the same thing in a very different context, where it would have taken on a different meaning. For example, say he had attended one of my little league baseball games where a controversial call by one of the umpires may have cost one team an important victory. With passions running high, some parents might get into shouting matches and perhaps even a couple of fists would fly. On the way home we kids might have asked, "Dad, why didn't you say anything when the other parents were arguing over that call? Other parents were really angry, but you just sat there." At such an imaginary moment, my father could have told us, *"¡En boca cerrada no entran moscas!"* In this different context, far removed from the family dinner table, the proverb would have taught us that sometimes it's better to keep one's mouth closed, to avoid jumping into an unproductive argument and potentially ending up in a bad or embarrassing situation.

Proverbs in a Collection Are Dead

Proverbs depend on a real-life situation to infuse them with meaning, which leads to another crucial observation: "A proverb in a collection is dead!"—or so proclaimed Wolfgang Mieder, one of the most prominent modern students of proverbs.[5] Mieder's assertion of the demise of collected sayings is a corollary to the idea we just discussed, namely that proverbs come to life when we speak and hear and understand them in specific times and places. "*¡En boca cerrada no entran moscas!*" meant something particularly clear when it was addressed to me and my siblings by our annoyed father. It functioned as a kind of "command" for us to be quiet. Apart from our dinner table, that imaginary little league baseball game, or some other oral context that can lend it meaning or life, however, it is a relatively unremarkable statement of fact: *Of course* nothing will enter a *closed* mouth! Proverbs in written collections—divorced from their use in real life—may be interesting, and we may appreciate their pithy and clever use of language, yet they tend to fall flat.

Every year when I teach my introductory course on the Hebrew Bible, I ask my students to read the Book of Proverbs straight through. Then I ask them afterward, "How was it? What did you think?" The response is remarkably similar year to year. The first student to speak is hesitant. "Well ... the first part (the poems of Proverbs 1–9) was kind of interesting...." Then with a bit more energy a second student interjects, "I recognized some of the proverbs ... but ... uhmm ... I really couldn't make it through the whole book." And then, with an animation born of frustration, a third student proclaims, on behalf of most others, "It just got too boring reading all those proverbs, one after another. I thought it would never end!"

This raises a key issue: How are we going to be able to mine the insights on money and economics that the sayings of the Book of Proverbs preserve, if these are entombed by the very pages upon which they are written?

Recontextualizing Proverbs

In one of his fantastic visions, the prophet Ezekiel witnessed a vast valley full of dry bones. In Ezekiel 37:3 the God of Israel asked him,

"O mortal, can these bones live?" Later, in the same verse, the prophet responded, shrewdly perhaps, "O, Lord God, you know." As we encounter the sayings in the Book of Proverbs, we must similarly ask, "Can these dead proverbs live again?" Perhaps only God knows for sure, but I am convinced that the answer is yes.

One way that the proverbs in a written collection, such as the Book of Proverbs, might live again is through what biblical scholar Diane Bergant has called a process of "recontextualization."[6] For Bergant, recontextualization essentially means that as we read the Book of Proverbs today, we look for those moments and places in our everyday lives when we might *speak* afresh the now *written* and dormant sayings of the ancient text.

Imagine, for example, that you encounter a coworker who is angry because she did not receive an expected promotion that carried a nice increase in salary. You know she was passed over because of her lackadaisical attitude on the job and her tendency to linger in conversation over the water cooler and in the lunchroom. In such a moment, having mined the sayings of the Book of Proverbs for their wisdom, you might exhort her with the words of Proverbs 14:23, "In all toil is profit, but mere talk makes only for lack." This, in essence, is the kind of "recontextualization" that Bergant (and others) promotes. A proverb from the collection of sayings in the Book of Proverbs is lifted off the written page and spoken afresh in a real-world context where it again "comes alive." In this potentially volatile moment, before speaking you might also do well to counsel yourself with the words of Proverbs 15:1, "A soft answer turns away wrath, but a harsh word stirs up anger."

This way of reanimating the biblical proverbs has several things to recommend it. For one thing it approximates the way people from various cultures actually use proverbs—to instruct, to command, to illustrate, and so on. Like my father, who knew how and when to use the Mexican proverb *"¡En boca cerrada no entran moscas!"* this way of using the biblical proverbs parallels how proverbs are used by most of us. It is also the way some folks, especially those who are biblically literate, draw on the wisdom of Proverbs today.

Recontextualizing Difficulties

"Recontextualization" is thus one way that we might reanimate the sayings of the Book of Proverbs, but it is not the best route to uncover Proverbs' teaching about money and the way of wisdom for us today. Indeed it has significant drawbacks. It depends on knowing—by memory—many of the hundreds of proverbs in the Book of Proverbs. Yet more and more people in North America make use of proverbs less and less. We no longer have the mind for proverbs the way our grandparents and others from an earlier generation or from other cultures do. Most people who speak the sayings of the Book of Proverbs today rely on only a handful of oft-quoted verses (such as "Trust in the Lord with all your heart and lean not on your understanding" [Proverbs 3:5]).

Of course, reading a collection of proverbs, making a conscious effort to remember them so they're available for use in a real-life situation, is also not how people generally learn and make use of proverbs. No, the manner in which we acquire and learn how to use proverbs is a much more subtle, even organic, process than rote memorization and recall. Some of us, for example, might be able to recall when we first worked to memorize a certain important piece of scripture. But do you remember when you first learned the saying "A bird in the hand is worth two in the bush"?

When thinking about how and whether the recontextualizing method might actually work in real life, it's also important to remember something else. Many biblical scholars are keen to compare the proverbs from the Bible with the proverbs of agrarian, preliterate African societies. However, other commentators note that the sayings of the Book of Proverbs are of a slightly different order than the proverbs of these cultures (as well as the proverbs some of us continue to use in our everyday lives).[7] There is a difference between the Igbo (Nigerian) saying "Drink is the molder of words" and, for instance, Proverbs 11:18, which claims, "The wicked earn no real gain (or wealth), but those who sow righteousness get a true reward," or Proverbs 28:11, which says, "The rich person is wise in his own eyes, but a discerning poor person searches him out."

The Igbo saying is the kind of short, pithy, and colorful saying that carries a general truth, as discussed above. It is a good example of the kind of proverb that folklorists record, collect, and study. You might imagine that it describes the way a little alcohol can sometimes loosen the tongue. But it could be used in a number of ways and in a number of contexts. It could be spoken to explain, more or less neutrally, another person's behavior ("Why is she going on and on about this topic?"—"Drink is the molder of words."). But it might also be used to pass a negative judgment on someone's behavior or to warn of the dangers of indiscretion that can accompany alcohol consumption ("Why is he saying *that* ... *to us* ... *about them* ...?"—"Drink is the molder of words."). In its translated form, moreover, it could even be used positively to praise a lover's heartfelt words, inspired by the consumption of spirits. In short, the Igbo proverb might be used the way many people use the Latin phrase *In vino veritas* ("In wine is truth") or the proverb, "Children and drunks always speak the truth!"[8]

The two sayings from the Book of Proverbs, by contrast, have more of a literary flavor. They are longer, and each is evenly balanced, employing opposite terms in each half of the verse: The wicked is contrasted to the righteous; the rich to the poor. The language in the sayings from Proverbs is also more morally charged than the language of the Igbo saying. In the Igbo saying, we need to imagine a larger oral context to figure out if the saying is being used to offer a negative, positive, or neutral judgment. The sayings from Proverbs include language that carries clear positive and negative connotations. Hence it is easier to see what values or virtues the proverb is promoting: what the righteous and discerning poor person does is obviously positive and good while the conduct of the wicked and the haughty rich person ("wise in his own eyes") is judged negatively.

The recontextualization method is thus limited by the difficulty of the task of learning so many new proverbs and by the fact that many of us no longer have a "mind" for proverbs. It is also limited because the more literary proverbs from the Book of Proverbs are of a slightly different order than the sorts of oral proverbs with which people in different times and places season their speech. In short, the method won't help us get very far into the subtleties of Proverbs' teaching about money and the way of wisdom. To get to that, we need to understand and embrace the *Book* of Proverbs, including its large collection of "dead" proverbs as precisely that: a book, a *literary* artifact.

Proverbs in the Book of Proverbs

If a proverb in a collection is dead, the proverbs of the Book of Proverbs have thus been transmitted to us postmortem, so to speak. How then are we to tap the sages' understanding about money and wisdom? We might try to imagine an original context for the sayings, to take a kind of educated guess as to how and when they might have been used by people in ancient Israel. This is not a bad strategy, and it is one that many biblical scholars employ in different ways.[9]

However, an educated guess is still just a guess. Given the limitations of recontextualization and the uncertainties of conjecture, it is ultimately best to attempt to understand the sayings of the Book of Proverbs in light of a different kind of context, namely, their *literary* context. We can best glean the meaning of the different sayings in Proverbs not by reapplying them to contemporary oral contexts, or by imagining some hypothetical original oral context, but by studying how the Book of Proverbs itself directs us and gives us clues as to what the different sayings mean.

This way of proceeding is possible because all proverbs, from the Bible's to Benjamin Franklin's, preserve and promote important values and virtues of a society or subculture. We can thus trace the values and virtues that the ancient sages of Proverbs wanted to pass on to us by paying close attention to the precise language the proverbs use and especially by attending to how and when they are employed in the ancient text itself. Even sayings about complex phenomena like money and morality that seem to contradict one another and that appear to promote very different kinds of behaviors can be analyzed to reveal how they fit into the larger system of values reflected in the Book of Proverbs.

We will soon turn to an in-depth study of the wisdom that Proverbs can offer us today about money and economics. However, first we must understand a little bit more about the ancient Hebrew book itself—who wrote it and when, how it was put together, and especially the ways it helps guide us to an understanding of the wisdom it presents to us. Proverbs' teaching about money and wisdom is subtle and profound. It offers us not merely antiquarian advice about how to "get more" but invites us to think seriously about how our money, and how we manage it, might accord (or not) with the wisdom that the sages claim is built into the very fabric of creation.

CHAPTER 2

Understanding the Book of Proverbs

Just as it is impossible to completely understand the Declaration of Independence without knowing something about Thomas Jefferson, the year 1776, and the fight against "taxation without representation," so, too, to understand the wisdom of Proverbs, we need to understand the context from which it sprang as well as who wrote the ancient text, and when and how it was organized or structured as a book. Within this literary context, we can begin to grasp the advice about money and the way of wisdom the sayings of the Book of Proverbs carry and what insights they might yield when it comes to dealing with our money. Because we live in a wired capitalist economy the likes of which the ancients could never have imagined—a world where with the click of a computer mouse huge amounts of capital can flow to the four corners of the world and fortunes can be won and lost—seeing beneath the surface "advice" of the sages will allow us to more faithfully engage the principles they promote and help us understand what is required of us to walk the way of wisdom in our own time and place.

Who Wrote Proverbs? And When?

God gave Solomon very great wisdom.
He was wiser than anyone else.
He composed three thousand proverbs.
(1 Kings 4:29, 31–32 [NRSV])

The legendary wisdom of King Solomon and the traditional belief
that he coined thousands of proverbs is celebrated in these verses
from 1 Kings. It is no surprise, then, that the "wisdom book" of
Proverbs is traditionally thought to have been written by Solomon
himself. The very first line of Proverbs (1:1) clearly links the book
with this ancient monarch: "The proverbs of Solomon son of David,
King of Israel." Biblical scholars, however, have long debated
whether this verse means that Solomon is the actual author of the
book, or if it merely suggests something less formal than authorship,
such as Solomonic "sponsorship" of the book's poems and sayings,
or simply some general association of the book with the legendary
wise king. As we saw in chapter 1, throughout history and across
cultures, proverbs and wise sayings have often been associated with
renowned individuals.

Proverbs itself actually cites at least two other wise individuals,
besides Solomon, as responsible for some of the material in the book.
In 30:1 a certain Agur is mentioned:

The words of Agur son of Jakeh. An oracle. Thus says the
man: I am weary, O God, I am weary, O God. How can I
prevail? (NRSV)

In 31:1, the mother of a certain King Lemuel:

The words of King Lemuel. An oracle that his mother taught him. (NRSV)

The different poems and proverbs in Proverbs were likely collected over a long period by learned Jewish scribes and sages who took care to preserve much of the ancient wisdom of their people. Like an imprimatur, King Solomon's name at the opening of Proverbs associates the entire book with the wise king, and assures readers that the wisdom and insights in its pages are reliable and valuable.

If King Solomon was in fact the author of Proverbs, then the book was written sometime around the middle of the tenth century BCE, the approximate period of his reign over Israel. However, if the poems and sayings of Proverbs were not actually written by Solomon, but only attributed to him, as is more likely, the question of the date of Proverbs gets a bit trickier. That would mean that different sections of the book were probably composed at different times, growing over time into the shape we find in our Bibles today.

Most biblical scholars agree that the earliest sections of Proverbs in all likelihood were not drawn together before the eighth century BCE, roughly the same time that the great Israelite prophets Hosea, Micah, Isaiah, and especially Amos were preaching against economic injustices in their society. The book did not take its final shape, however, until the period between the end of the Babylonian exile in 539 BCE, when the Persian empire began to rule over the Jewish homeland, and the rise of the Greeks under Alexander the Great in 333 BCE, who likewise dominated the ancient world of the Jews. The late fifth or early fourth century BCE are relatively safe guesses for the establishment of the final form of the Hebrew Book of Proverbs.

When we reflect on what Proverbs says to us today about wealth and poverty, it will sometimes be helpful to recall the real-life economic pressures people were experiencing at the hands of oppressive elites and exploitive empires when the book's sayings were penned. By recalling such matters, we might be able to draw helpful analogies between their time and place and our own; or we might better recognize how different the world of Proverbs is from our world and thereby avoid the pitfalls of simplistically "translating" their words directly into our culture. Both sorts of insights can help us home in on Proverbs' wisdom about money and riches for us today, to figure out what from the world of Proverbs is applicable to ours. Indeed, although the world of the sages of Proverbs was in many respects vastly different from ours—they lived under a monarchy in a predominantly agricultural society, for example—in other ways, their concerns are remarkably analogous to our own.

For example, just as the economic decisions and priorities of ancient Israel were often foisted on the Israelites by inaccessible, far-off imperial powers—Assyria, Babylon, and Persia—so, too, some of us sense that our own economic well-being is determined by forces beyond our control. The trade representatives who negotiate treaties like NAFTA (the North American Free Trade Agreement), which hinder or facilitate the outsourcing of jobs, do so in closed sessions. The legislators who write and rewrite tax laws and regulate (or not) mortgage and financial markets are cloistered in Washington, D.C., far from our everyday lives. Our retirement savings, and the future quality of life they represent, are subjected to the whims of financial markets that no one seems to truly understand and that very often have different priorities than we do. Hence, although the details may differ, both the sages and we can recognize that our actions concerning our money are governed by a larger, often impersonal, system.

How Is Proverbs Structured?

The ancient sages crafted the Book of Proverbs purposively, and their careful editorial work reflects the integrity of the Book of

Proverbs as a whole. To fully grasp Proverbs' ancient wisdom about wealth and poverty for our own lives, it is also important to know something about the book's literary organization, for the very structure of the book affects its meaning. Understanding the work's structure reveals how one part of the book or one group of proverbs is related to, and can help to interpret, others that may sound very different. This enables us to see the literary context of Proverbs within which the sayings about wealth and poverty are best understood.

For instance, Proverbs is divided neatly into two major sections. The first part, chapters 1–9, consists of long, well-crafted poems that speak quite generally of "two ways" in life: the "way" of wisdom and the "way" of folly. These chapters, which prepare us for the more specific instruction of the short proverbs later in the book, also describe two women—Woman Wisdom and the "strange" or "foreign" woman, identified as Woman Folly (Proverbs 9:13, p. 45)—who personify the two "ways."[1] The second main section of Proverbs consists of chapters 10–31, which are composed of lists of short sentences or sayings, what we popularly refer to as proverbs. Certain motifs introduced in the first part of the book, such as the "two ways" and the sages' strong belief in the value of virtue, are carried through and modified to some extent in the second part of the book.

Besides the major division between chapters 1–9 and 10–31, several other subsections in Proverbs are indicated by distinct "superscriptions," or headings, that are part of the book itself. For example, Proverbs 25:1 tells us that the short sayings following that verse are "the proverbs of Solomon that the officials of King Hezekiah of Judah copied." What's more, in chapter 31 the first nine verses appear to be the words of the mother of a certain King Lemuel whom we mentioned above, while the final lines of that chapter (verses 10–31) seem to comprise an independent poem, composed in acrostic style (each line begins with a successive letter of the Hebrew alphabet), extolling the virtues of the so-called woman of worth or woman of valor—in Hebrew, the *eshet hayil*. Hence, just as the first section of the book, chapters 1–9, speaks of two women, so the final section highlights two women. We will look at each of these sections in subsequent chapters.

We should also recall that, unlike modern collections of proverbs gathered by folklorists—those collections of English or African-American, Old Irish or Mexican sayings, for example—which simply list, one after another, the hundreds and hundreds of spoken proverbs of a given people or culture, the proverbs in the Book of Proverbs comprise an *intentional* collection of sayings of the ancient Israelites. The sages and scribes who composed the book, did not write down for us *all* the proverbial wisdom of their people. Moreover, although scholars continue to debate the extent to which the ancient scribes intentionally organized the sayings in Proverbs 10–29, it is clear that they carefully chose and often artfully arranged the sayings they preserved in order to emphasize the themes and lessons they wanted us to hear. Most commentators agree that some proverbs, for instance, are grouped together because they share a common theme or vocabulary, or because they use words that in Hebrew share similar sounds. And some sayings are positioned in a particular place in the collection to offer a comment on the proverbs that surround it.

Guides to Understanding

Yet despite its intentional structure, the Book of Proverbs can still be very difficult to get into, as many of my students have observed. Its lists of proverb after proverb can be discouraging, even for the most determined of readers. Fortunately, it seems that the ancient sages who put the Book of Proverbs together anticipated this problem, creating "guides" to help us through the material.

Our First Guide to Understanding: The Prologue

The most important of these guides is the Prologue,[2] an introduction to the book, which helps us understand how to interpret it. The very first line of Proverbs serves as the title of the book,[3] but the next six verses (2–7) form the Prologue proper. These lines tell us three key things: (1) the purpose of the book; (2) how it's going to instruct us, the book's readers; and (3) who the book was written for. Let's look at each in turn.

The Prologue of Proverbs (1:2–7) reads:

> [2]For learning about wisdom and instruction, for understanding words of insight,
>> [3]for gaining instruction in wise dealing, righteousness, justice, and equity;
> [4]to teach shrewdness to the simple, knowledge and prudence to the young;
> [5]Let the wise also hear and gain in learning, and the discerning acquire skill,
> [6]to understand a proverb and a figure, the words of the wise and their riddles.
> [7]The fear of the Lord is the beginning of knowledge; fools despise wisdom and instruction. (NRSV)

What do we learn from these lines? In what sense can the Prologue serve us as a "guide" to understanding and interpreting the poems and proverbs that follow?

The first thing that we learn from verses 2–4 of the Prologue is what the book is going to be about and why it was written; we learn its *purpose*—what kinds of wisdom and what sorts of values, virtues, and character traits the book will be passing on and promoting. For example, verse 2 tells us that the book hopes to pass on to its readers what I call *intellectual virtues*. It speaks of "wisdom" and "under-standing words of insight"—in other words, the things we do with our minds, such as study, reflect, and decide to tell the truth (or not) in a given situation. Verse 4 tells us that the book wants to instruct us in "shrewdness" and "prudence," or in what might be called *practical virtues*. These are the particular strategies by which we choose to live our lives and through which we express our commitments and desires; for instance, cultivating relationships with coworkers and superiors with an eye toward advancing in our field or profession.

Verse 3, however, is somewhat distinct from verses 2 and 4. It speaks of "wise dealing" but then immediately defines this wise deal-ing by mentioning three important terms—*justice, righteousness,* and *equity*—words that elsewhere in the Bible have to do with social justice, especially economic justice. This is a central clue to another kind of virtue the book will discuss, what I call *social virtue,* and this is most important for our study.

Much like the messages of the prophets mentioned above, Proverbs has a kind of prophetic core—it challenges some of our most cherished assumptions and beliefs regarding money, its accu-mulation, and our sense of what our obligation to others with less ought to be. Often it accomplishes this profound mission in surpris-ingly subtle ways. The terminology of *justice* and *righteousness* in verse 3, for example, appears regularly in the preaching of the great Israelite prophets like Isaiah, Micah, and Amos—all of whom preached that the plight of the poor and marginalized in ancient Israel had to be addressed and mitigated.[4] These prophets, recall, were also active in the eighth century BCE, the same time that the earliest sec-tions of Proverbs were being composed and collected. Verse 3 of Proverbs' Prologue thus tells us that the book will be promoting and passing on to us the importance of these great themes, which preoc-cupied the greatest prophets of that age. In fact Proverbs 21:3, "To do righteousness and justice is more desirable to the Lord than sacrifice" (NRSV) sounds like it could have been uttered by Amos (Amos 4:4–5) or Isaiah (Isaiah 1:10–20)[5].

The central importance of this prophetic core of Proverbs is highlighted even in the literary design of the Prologue, where verse 3 stands at the pinnacle of a particular poetic structure. The poetic arrangement of the verses is easier to see in Hebrew than in English, but I have tried to represent it in the text above by indenting verse 3. The poetic structure of the Prologue indicates that the social virtues of verse 3 were paramount to the sages. They have a preeminent place in the hierarchy of values that one can discern in the book and in a sense serve as a norm against which all the book's teaching about money and riches, the poor and poverty must measure up. By virtue of its position at the end of the Prologue, many scholars believe that verse 7 also articulates something crucial to the sages' moral imagination. It expresses the book's "motto," reflecting one of Proverb's central values—reverence for the divine.

The second thing the Prologue teaches us, in verses 5 and 6, is *how* the book is going to instruct us. In particular, verse 6 mentions that the book's instruction is going to be offered through not merely "wise words" but "proverbs," "figures," and "riddles." In the Bible all three of these terms are used in passages that are full of figurative language.[6] The terms reveal that such passages are in need of some sort of interpretation. The Prologue thus also tells us, right at the outset, that we need to expect that some of the instruction in Proverbs may, at moments, prove a little difficult to grasp.

Finally the Prologue as a whole also tells us *who* the book of Proverbs was written *for*. Verse 3 mentions that the book's instruction is for simpletons and youth, two groups who would obviously be in need of the sages' wise lessons. But verse 5 also mentions the "wise person" and the one with some "understanding" as those who may learn something from the book. Scholars usually suggest that the Prologue is thus telling us that "anyone" can learn from Proverbs. Whether you are young and uneducated or old and full of the gray hair that wisdom brings, there is something here for you.

So Proverbs is written for both the young and simple and the old and wise. But the Prologue may also be telling us that those who want to learn from the Book of Proverbs should act like one who is in need of instruction (the simple youth) and like one who is wise, ready to engage the work of interpreting proverbs, figures, and riddles—work that will require some intellectual effort. In fact, in the pages that follow the Prologue, the kind of people the sages originally imagined addressing appear neither as young children nor as wise sages, but as young adult men.[7]

Why does Proverbs address young men? The ancient world, including the world of the Bible, was very patriarchal. As we will see, the imaginations of the sages, who were products of their time and culture, were limited in this and other ways, and in this regard at times failed to fully live up to the vision of justice and equity (cf. 1:3, p. 23) toward which their teaching points. Nevertheless, by calling attention to their shortcomings in this regard and recognizing that we today need not be bound by the social strictures of the sages' society, both men and women in the contemporary world can learn from their wisdom.

Our Second Guide to Understanding: The Two "Ways"

The sages who composed Proverbs not only gave us the Prologue as a guide to interpreting the book, they also crafted its poems and sayings, including its proverbs about money and economics, in a manner that helps us recognize the fundamental lessons they wanted us to hear and understand. One of the most important techniques they used to achieve this was the metaphor of the "way" and "walking the way" to talk about the values, virtues, and behaviors that lead to a good and flourishing life.

For the sages of Proverbs the world was divided into two possible paths, the *way of wisdom* and righteousness on the one hand, and the *way of folly* and wickedness on the other. If you read carefully and keep an eye out for it, you will find the metaphor of the way used throughout Proverbs, though it is especially common in chapters 1–9. This means that whatever is described positively as righteous and wise, at any point in the book, belongs to the *way of wisdom* and that which is described negatively as wicked and foolish, anywhere in the book, belongs to the *way of folly*. The readers of the book, including us today, are invited to choose between the two ways. Particularly when it comes to how we think and then act with our money, we need to ask ourselves: Will we choose the way of wisdom or the path of folly?

An Introductory Vignette—Proverbs 1:10–19

The choice between the two ways, however, is not as simple as you might expect, for it involves more than electing for simple reward or avoiding simple punishment. As in life, the way of wisdom does not always appear as attractive as the way of folly. This is clearest in Proverbs 1:10–19, just after the Prologue concludes. Here the sages offer an initial vignette that shows the motif of the "two ways" in action and affirms the idea that the "wrong way" can often appear very appealing. It also offers us our first practical lessons about money and the way of wisdom—a kind of cautionary tale.

> [10]My child, if sinners entice you, do not consent.
> [11]If they say, "Come with us, let us lie in wait for blood; let us wantonly ambush the innocent;
> [12]like Sheol let us swallow them alive and whole, like those who go down to the Pit.

¹³We shall find all kinds of costly things; we shall fill our houses with booty.

¹⁴Throw in your lot among us; we will all have one purse"—

¹⁵my child, do not walk in their way, keep your foot from their paths;

¹⁶for their feet run to evil, and they hurry to shed blood.

¹⁷For in vain is the net baited while the bird is looking on;

¹⁸yet they lie in wait—to kill themselves! and set an ambush—for their own lives!

¹⁹Such is the end of all who are greedy for gain; it takes away the life of its possessors. (NRSV)

In verses 10–14 of this passage, the reader, who is addressed by a father (or a teacher), as a son (or a student), is initially enticed by "sinners" who are described as murderous robbers.[8] The robbers promise that if the son joins up with them he will receive "all kinds of costly things," or simply "all precious wealth" (from the Hebrew *kol hon yaqar*), and enough to fill up all their houses (verse 13). The sinners hope, and perhaps know from experience, that they will in fact gain financially from their thievery. They also know that the "son" who hears this promise of riches will find it attractive. The robbers know the allure of money. And they know that the "son" knows it, too. Thus they dangle the promise of material gain in front of the son, as a way to tempt him to join them. To follow the sinners' way, the son is promised money—lots of it.

But notice how the father, or the instructing voice of the teacher, responds with a metaphorical language for morality. He tells the son not to "walk" in the "way" of the robbers and to keep his "foot" far from their "paths" (verse 15). Their way, which they are so eager to pursue (verse 16; "their feet run" and "they hurry"), is not the right way; it is not the way of wisdom and righteousness. This is clear because it is associated with Sheol and the Pit, two designations for the netherworld in ancient Israel. It is described too as the way of "sinners" (verse 10) and as a path that is "evil" and violent unto death (verse 16). It is, in short, the way of folly and wickedness. Even so, one gets the distinct impression from the passage that the temptation to grab hold of such "precious wealth" may prove too great for the son.

But consider how the teaching voice of the father unmasks as a lie the robbers' promise of "all precious wealth," and how he counters their claims. The teacher claims that the robbers, in fact, will not find "all precious wealth" at all, but rather something very different, what in Hebrew he calls *batsaʿ*. The NRSV translates the phrase *botseaʿ batsaʿ* as "greedy for gain" (verse 19). Yet the root of these two related Hebrew terms in the Bible is often associated with injustice. Hence, the father or teacher claims that the robbers' offer is not one of "all precious wealth" as in verse 13, but what he renames "unjust gain" in verse 19." Yet more than this, he asserts that the sinners' quest for gain will lead not to wealth but to their own death. He says that, while the robbers in seeking their own profit lie in wait to murder *others* (verses 11–12), they ironically actually threaten their *own* lives (verse 19).

By renaming the loot the robbers hope to gain, the father is picking up on the robbers' own rhetoric or their own way of describing their deeds. Recall that earlier they talked about filling their houses with "booty" (verse 13). The term "booty" or *spoil* (Hebrew *shalal*) is a term that is often associated with war and warriors. "To the victors (in any battle), go the spoils," as the saying goes. Although in war there is routinely a political justification and a kind of warrior's code that attempts to legitimize the seizing of booty by violence, the robbers in Proverbs 1 are not soldiers in a battle; they are those who attack the *innocent* and brutally overwhelm them. The martial language underscores that the robbers gain their loot by unjustified violence. By having the robbers themselves utter such words, the sages hint that the sinners already have an implicit sense of the wrongness of their way of seeking gain.

Rethinking Prosperity

There are several things in this first vignette in Proverbs that can help us better understand the book's wisdom teachings when it comes to money and riches. First of all, we learn that the Book of Proverbs knows very well the real worth or allure of money in the real world. Then, as now, money holds powerful sway over the human imagination. But more important, as the Prologue tells us to expect, we see already in the very first episode of the book that the sages of Proverbs can, at least in part, deploy the language of wealth to talk to us in an imaginative or figurative way about how valuable something else, some noneconomic good, might be. Specifically we learn that Proverbs can use talk of money to express how valuable a certain "way" of life is, or, in the case of the robbers' "wrong way," how valuable a particular way might appear to be. These fundamental insights regarding how the sages use language will help us understand other wealth and poverty sayings later in Proverbs.

Yet the passage can also teach us some important moral lessons about money and wealth today. Like the robbers of Proverbs, some of us today are also often tempted to follow the wrong way with the hope of acquiring something that we desire and know to be of real worth—"all precious wealth." Like the one addressed in Proverbs 1, some of us also mistakenly think that our quest for wealth will yield a fulfilling and happy life, when in reality that very quest undermines our efforts at achieving a meaningful and good life. As Albert

Einstein, the great and wise physicist, once noted, "Human beings can attain a worthy and harmonious life only if they are able to rid themselves ... of the striving for the wish fulfillment of material kinds."[9]

This first passage in Proverbs also teaches us that the sages of old did not equate the acquisition of money or wealth *by any means* as automatically being a good thing. The passage teaches us that gaining wealth through schemes that attack and violently take advantage of others is *not* the way of wisdom; rather, it belongs to the way of wickedness. On one level, this may seem self-evident to any decent person, and certainly most of us are not violent criminals. We would never entertain the idea of using brute, physical force ourselves to rob another of her possessions. Yet the robbers in chapter 1 are not merely literal robbers. Because they are presented to us at the beginning of the book, their obvious wicked character shows them to be something like a symbol for all that belongs to the way of folly. This insight, much like the insight offered by the Prologue, invites us to think critically (intellectual virtue) about how the vignette about violent robbers might have something to say to us today about economic justice (social virtue), and how we might take action to see that justice is actually realized (practical virtue).

The sages' words can serve as an invitation for us to consider how even our legitimate quests for money, and the things that money can buy us, might incur violence against others, even if that violence is hidden or indirect. To what extent, for instance, are our new, affordable clothes bought at the price of sweatshop labor that exploits poor workers, including children, in developing countries? Before the high-profile revelation in the 1990s that television personality Kathy Lee Gifford's line of clothes was manufactured in sweatshop conditions (and often by young children), such far-reaching consequences of low retail prices were largely unknown to most

American consumers. Even now, such practices continue, but surely the sages would agree that awareness of the problem is at least a small first step in the right direction.

We might also ask to what extent our rich, varied, and affordable food is acquired at the cost of trade agreements that force small, struggling farmers off their land, even if most of us don't do anything directly to set things up that way? To what extent do our investments, which are supposed to "make money" for us, depend for their success on global economic arrangements that favor both rich countries and the wealthy of every country?

But we are not left to ponder such fundamental ethical questions alone, or weigh our responses in a vacuum. Many individuals, and more and more businesses have also begun to take stock of such questions. The fair trade movement, for instance, aims to overturn centuries of exploitation by ensuring that farmers in developing countries receive a fair wage for the products they ship overseas, particularly for consumable items, such as coffee, tea, and chocolate.[10] Once mainly the purview of specialty or gourmet shops and small companies such as Vermont-based Green Mountain Coffee Roasters or New Orleans' Orleans Coffee Roasters, fair trade items can now be purchased in some of America's largest franchises, including Starbucks and Wal-Mart. Buying fair trade products is one small way that we can take up the challenge that the sages' words in Proverbs 1 set before us. It is one strategy by which we might begin to walk wisdom's way of justice.

But it is only one small step. The sages' prophetic impulse will not permit us to rest on our laurels of learning about injustice or on important, but small and generally not very costly gestures, like buying fair trade products. They ask us rather to push ahead and make further use of our intellectual and practical virtues to think about what we might next do. Yes, we are now offered fair trade coffee at

Starbucks. But according to the Organic Consumers Association only about 3.7 percent of all the coffee sold at Starbucks is fair trade, and in the world market an equally tiny percentage of coffee is sold fair trade. This means that countless numbers of coffee growers and harvesters worldwide remain in precarious economic positions.[11] The first step on the way of wisdom can never be the last.

The sages, however, will not permit us to merely condemn as hopelessly corrupt systems and structures that have advanced injustice, without seriously considering what these systems and structures do well and to understand how they might be, or might become, genuine tools to promote justice and the common good. The sages hold their prophetic and critical-practical vocations together. They ask us to do the same. Indeed, how much farther down wisdom's path would we collectively travel if, for example, the largest retailers in the United States could be convinced to dedicate not some tiny percentage of their retail stock to fair trade products, but turned their attention more fully to the principles of the fair trade movement to help establish living wages and reduce inequities both here and abroad? How might the clout of a Starbucks or a Wal-Mart, if they insisted on fair trade policies for all their products, change the very structure of current profit-dominated business models across the board?

The initial vignette of Proverbs also offers us another lesson. Recall that the sinners believed they were chasing something good and valuable, "precious wealth." However, the sinners' quest turned out to be a pursuit of "unjust gain" that was not only going to cost the lives of their victims, but their own lives as well. The initial story about the robbers thus reminds us of how, for some of us, the anxious pursuit of wealth is not providing us with more, but rather less, well-being. Do you work sixty hours a week to pay the bills? Do you feel as if you are sacrificing a more genuine and comfortable life because you feel compelled to maintain a lifestyle that is beyond your means? Do the day-to-day details of your life align with the overall direction and orientation you want your life to have? These are the sorts of questions the sages would have us ask ourselves.

Upon reflection, we also notice that besides teaching us something about the potentially high personal cost of pursuing money, the first vignette of Proverbs also helps us see and understand that the possession of money and wealth is not a clear-cut automatic sign—to ourselves or to others—that we are on the right path. It is not a clear-cut sign of wisdom and righteousness, or divine favor.

This observation is important because many people today *do* equate gaining wealth with God's favor or as a sign of some spiritual or moral superiority. This is particularly true of some Christians who adhere to what is sometimes called the "prosperity gospel." The basic idea of the prosperity gospel is that God wants us all to prosper economically. Then economic status is viewed as a sign of spiritual and moral favor from God. If you have a lot of money, God is blessing you. If you don't, you are obviously not trusting God enough, or you are not conforming your life sufficiently to the divine will. Although God certainly desires good things for all God's creatures, prosperity gospel thinking skews the idea of *well-being* in a crass economic direction.

In the nonreligious, secular realm, the idea of a prosperity gospel has its counterpart in the ideology of capitalism and the American Dream, which claims that if you only work hard enough, you will make it; you will be able to earn and enjoy "all precious wealth."

The problem with this sort of prosperity gospel thinking, whether in its religious or secular version, is that it begins to confuse the way of wisdom and the way of folly, so that those who do not succeed economically are labeled by some as religiously or morally inferior. "They don't trust God enough"; or "they are lazy and not truly working hard," or at least not hard enough. Yet, this way of thinking does not hold true in many instances. For example, you probably know, or know of, very religious and pious people whose faith in the Divine is firm, or people who, in pursuing the American Dream, work terribly hard. But these pious people and hardworking people still struggle to get ahead economically. The sages, too, knew that wealth and wisdom don't necessarily run parallel. Recall Proverbs 28:11, which was quoted above: "The rich person is wise in his own eyes, but a discerning poor person searches him out."

Our experience also shows us that some of those who advocate prosperity gospel thinking (whether the religious or secular variety) themselves turn out to be on the path of folly. One such example involved televangelist Robert Tilton, who in the 1980s built an extraordinarily popular television ministry in which he frequently solicited large financial donations from his viewers in return for prayers and promises of healing. But in 1991, ABC News investigated his ministry and exposed Tilton as a fraud and his ministry, which soon collapsed, as a farce. The claims he made to his viewers were so outlandish, and his utter disregard for the heartfelt responses that accompanied their donations so heartless (prayer requests were discarded without being read, for example) that the situation would have been comical if not for the many poor and vulnerable people who lost everything to his scam.

To the extent that we believe that the prosperity gospel way of thinking is true and understand ourselves to be prospering primarily because of our hardworking and spiritual or pious natures, we may be deceiving ourselves. By the sages' standard, we may even be on the way of folly. Some of us may, in fact, believe so much in the prosperity ideology that we can't see instances in our world where it simply is not true. We may unconsciously believe it to be true, or mostly true, in order to continue hoping that our prosperity will actually one day provide us with the fulfilling and meaningful lives we long for. We hold fast to this way of thinking to avoid asking ourselves the hard questions we began to ask above about how our prosperity might be bought, even indirectly, at a violent cost to others.

This is not to say that if we are prosperous, *some* part of our prosperity is not a result of our own hard work. It often is. It is simply to remind us that the prosperity gospel way of thinking provides inadequate explanation or moral justification for the economic inequalities in our world. It can't be used to make the sorts of judgments that say "these people are poor" because of some moral shortcoming and "these people are rich" because of some virtue—whether we are speaking of individuals, social classes or even nations.

Simply put, prosperity gospel thinking doesn't take into account where we start from. Many women and minorities, for instance, know firsthand that despite years of social advancement, social and economic opportunities are not equal for all. In the United States women, African Americans, and Hispanics continue, on average, to earn significantly less than white men do, often for the same work.[12] Likewise, many people in developing nations believe that no amount of hard work, economic structural adjustments, free trade agreements, or aid packages will easily or quickly reverse the effects of centuries of slavery and colonization. Why not? Because international economic policies still primarily serve the interests of rich nations over poor nations, as noted by several high-profile figures such as Nobel Laureate Joseph E. Stiglitz and maverick investor George Soros—simultaneously supporters and critics of global capitalism. Stiglitz writes, "The policies of the international economic institutions are all too often closely aligned with the commercial and financial interests of those in the advanced countries." Indeed, sometimes the effects of certain policies, Stiglitz notes, can leave a country "just as impoverished but with more debt and an even richer ruling elite."[13] Just as individuals don't start out on equal footing, neither do countries. As Soros opines, global economic processes "create a very uneven playing field."[14]

So as we consider our neighbors around the corner, around town, or around the globe, we need to remember this initial bit of wisdom from Proverbs: The possession of "precious wealth" or money is not necessarily a sign of blessing or virtue since it can be, and in the real world often is, the product of unjust gain. The hard part for any of us is to discern what of our gain is "unjust." The sages, however, ask us to honestly examine ourselves. Is our prosperity—personal and corporate—in line with wisdom's virtues and its emphasis on social virtue, or is our way a path that diverges from wisdom's way? Are our lives, including our financial lives, consistent with the way of folly, or are our actions and attitudes aligned with wisdom and justice?

Money and Valuable Wisdom in Proverbs 1–9

The sages used the Prologue to establish the book's purpose, and the first vignette both to offer some initial lessons about money and wisdom and to show how the book uses metaphorical language to communicate its message. But the Book of Proverbs by no means stops talking about money and the way of wisdom here. In the rest of chapters 1–9, the sages use a series of long, artful poems, to further develop and refine with increasing urgency their teaching about the relative worth of wisdom, folly, and money. All this, in turn, lays the interpretive foundation for understanding the short proverbs we encounter in the second part of the book, chapters 10–31.

In the poems following the initial vignette of Proverbs 1, the sages mention money or material wealth in at least six or seven different passages and continue to redefine for us what is of real value in life. It's not money, and the constant pursuit of more of it that is of great worth. It's the way of wisdom and virtue.

Pursue Wisdom as You Would Money—Proverbs 2:4–5

After the episode with the robbers in Proverbs 1:10–19 (see pp. 27–28), the next time the sages speak of money and wealth is in Proverbs 2:4–5. The sages tell us that if we pursue wisdom with the same passion and energy that many of us seek money and material wealth, we will certainly find it.

> [4]If you seek it [wisdom] like silver and search for it as for
>   a hidden treasure,
> [5]Then you will understand the fear of the Lord and find
>   the knowledge of God. (NRSV)

In analyzing these lines, notice first that, "fear of the Lord" and "knowledge of God" are virtues that belong to the way of wisdom. This is clear from the different ways Proverbs associates these virtues with wisdom and from the fact that the Prologue in 1:7 (see p. 23) highlights the "fear of the Lord" as the "beginning of wisdom." Here in chapter 2, the very next verse in the passage makes clear that all wisdom is from God: "For the Lord gives wisdom; from his mouth come knowledge and understanding" (Proverbs 2:6).

Second, contrary to the popular view that understanding Proverbs will lead to material wealth, these lines do *not* say that wisdom will bring you money or wealth. The passage doesn't even equate money and wisdom. It only says that you should pursue wisdom and virtue with the same zeal displayed by many of us who strive for money and financial security. This is the kind of energy and devotion Proverbs says we should use to pursue wisdom, including especially the virtue of social justice, which the book's Prologue highlights. The sages promise us that wisdom and virtue—not wealth—will produce the good and flourishing life we seek.

Third, at this point in the book, the sages of Proverbs begin to expand on their linguistic code when it comes to riches and poverty. They do not talk about money and wealth in precisely the same way that the "sinners" did in chapter 1. The sinners, recall, spoke of "booty," and precious wealth (*hon yaqar*) in more general terms. Here the sages speak of "silver" and "hidden treasures" in more specific terms. These are valuable material goods that one might passionately pursue, just as one might pursue other kinds of wealth and money. But the difference in terminology between the sinners in chapter 1 and the father or teacher here in chapter 2 is important. By speaking in specifics, the sages are redefining what is of genuine value in life. Using different, though related, money words to talk about how valuable wisdom is, they adopt the language of metaphor to convey their teachings.

One famous contemporary sage, His Holiness the Dalai Lama, has offered insight that resonates with the sages of Proverbs. He has said, "We feel money and power can bring happiness and solve problems, but they are not definite causes of those desired states." For the Dalai Lama, the key to a fulfilling life has to do not with money or its pursuit but with "a certain way of thinking" that "makes us happy," for there are certain "states of mind that bring us peace and happiness, and we need to cultivate and enhance" these.[15]

If we took the insights of the Dalai Lama and the sages of Proverbs to heart, we would discover that happiness is already at hand for those of us who already have enough money, and that striving less for contentment through material gain may be the key to finding it.

Imagine if we were to take seriously the sages' words about passionately pursuing wisdom and virtue. How would our lives change? Of course the sages of old knew that we all need to pursue a certain degree of material prosperity not merely to survive, but to thrive. But where is the line between "pursuing" and obsession? Where is the border between "enough" and "just a little more"? For the sages, we should be able to say "enough" when speaking about material wealth, but always seek "just a little more" when it comes to wisdom's virtues, like the justice and equity the sages speak of in Proverbs' Prologue.

Wisdom Is More Precious than Money—Proverbs 3:13–16

The next time the sages of Proverbs speak of wealth in relation to wisdom is in Proverbs 3:13–16. After the father or teacher instructs readers to guard carefully his instruction, to trust in the Lord, to honor the Lord through the giving of tithes, and to accept divine rebukes, these verses read:

> [13]Happy are those who find wisdom and those who get understanding
> [14]For her income is better than silver and her revenue better than gold
> [15]She is more precious than jewels and nothing you desire can compare with her.
> [16]Long life is in her right hand; in her left hand are riches and honor. (NRSV)

Here Proverbs states clearly that happiness or contentment in life belongs not to those who acquire more and more money and material goods, but to those who find wisdom (verse 13). Verse 14 states explicitly that wisdom is "better than" both silver and gold—the two metals that many of us still view as most valuable. But the passage goes on to say that wisdom is also "more precious" than jewels or anything else we might desire; it's more valuable than any other material good or any amount of money.

Interestingly, in verse 16 the sages say that in addition to "riches," wisdom—personified as a woman—holds in her hands "long life" and "honor." These three things—riches, honor, and long life—would, of course, have been very valuable to the ancient Israelites—the original audience of Proverbs. But today we also recognize the value of "riches," appreciate the "honor" and respect of friends and colleagues, and hope for a full, healthy, "long life."

The personification of wisdom in Proverbs begins in Proverbs 1:20, where wisdom "cries out" to passersby, trying to convince them to choose her "way."

> Wisdom cries out in the street; in the squares she raises her voice. (NRSV)

Many scholars believe that the personification of wisdom as a woman in Proverbs is modeled on the image of some ancient goddess. The Egyptian deities of Isis and Ma'at are sometimes mentioned as possible models, and Woman Wisdom does seem to bear a resemblance to certain ancient descriptions and depictions of both goddesses. Yet whatever the background of the figure of Woman Wisdom, in Proverbs she is primarily a personification of the wisdom of the Israelite God Yahweh.

Whether or not the figure of Woman Wisdom is modeled on an ancient goddess, the use of the literary device of personification is an indication that the sages are once again using metaphorical language to speak to us about the value of wisdom. Recall that the Prologue tells us that the book would use figurative language to teach us about wisdom's virtues. Just as 3:14–15 describe wisdom's worth by telling us that she is more valuable than gold and silver and jewels, the "riches" and "honor" and "long life" that wisdom holds in verse 16—symbols of the good and flourishing life that can be had by following wisdom's way—present us with yet another way to talk about wisdom's worth.

In Proverbs 3:13–16 the sages continue using a language of wealth and riches that is slightly different than that of the sinners in chapter 1. There is no talk of the sinners' "precious wealth" (*hon yaqar*), but of gold, silver, jewels and "riches" (*'osher*). The book is thus continuing to redefine for us what is of true value in life—wisdom rather than wealth—and it does so by using a range of different "wealth" terms to talk about how valuable wisdom is. This poetic redefinition and expansion of the meaning of *riches,* however, might also be said to be a subtle way the sages ask us today to think about the ways we overvalue all those things that we do not explicitly call our "money." It asks us, perhaps, to consider to what extent wisdom and virtue or our possessions—all those things that money buys, and not merely our bank balances—form the true object of our desires.

"Buy" Wisdom—Proverbs 4:5–7

The fourth chapter of Proverbs also begins with the father or teacher instructing his sons or pupils (verses 1–2). However, just as my father always prefaced his statements about flies not entering a closed mouth with the words, "As Grandpa Sandoval used to say ..." so, too, the teacher here grounds the authority of his instruction in the fact that he received this counsel from *his* parents, "When I was a son with my father, tender, and my mother's favorite" (Proverbs 4:3). Proverbs 4:5–7 then continues:

⁵Get wisdom; get insight: do not forget, nor turn away
from the words of my mouth.

⁶Do not forsake her, and she will keep you; love her, and she
will guard you.

⁷The beginning of wisdom is this: Get Wisdom, and whatever else you get, get insight (NRSV)

At first glance these lines don't seem to have much to do with the issue we have been exploring, namely, how the way of wisdom relates to money and wealth. However, a slightly different translation of certain terms in verses 5 and 7 reveals that these lines, too, are intimately related to our discussion.

⁵Buy wisdom; buy insight....

⁷The beginning of wisdom is this: Buy wisdom, and in
exchange for all your goods, buy insight!

In Hebrew the verb *qanah,* which can be translated as "get," as seen in the NRSV, sometimes also carries economic connotations. And in this context, it almost certainly has an economic overtone or nuance since in verse seven, the verb is followed in Hebrew by the proposition, *bet* ("by," "with"). In the Bible, when the verb *qanah* is followed by this preposition the two constitute an idiom of economic exchange that means "to buy." With this translation we can thus plainly hear the economic language, the language of money.

The verse is telling us to use whatever we have to "purchase" wisdom. Although in today's world you can surely buy certain forms of knowledge and instruction, obviously you can't literally buy wisdom. You don't find an intangible virtue or quality of character for sale in the marketplace. Rather, the sages are using figurative language to communicate their ideas. They are saying that the intangible virtue of wisdom is so valuable that, if we could, we should use *all* our money, *all* our possessions to acquire it.

The emphasis on wisdom's value is also reflected in the way the sages expand their range of vocabulary, but in a surprising direction. Verse 6 speaks of the desirability of wisdom, again personified, not just in terms of wealth, but in subtly erotic terms as well. The original male addressee of the book is first encouraged in verse 6 not to "forsake" wisdom, but to "love her." In verse 8 he is told that if he will "embrace" her, wisdom will bring him honor and place a "fair garland" or "beautiful crown" on his head.

> [8]Prize her highly, and she will exalt you; she will honor
> you if you embrace her.
> [9]She will place on your head a fair garland; she will
> bestow on you a beautiful crown (Proverbs 4:8–9;
> NRSV)

Many scholars believe that this sort of language is evocative of ancient marriages and wedding celebrations: The addressee is being encouraged to pursue wisdom as he might pursue a desirable bride.[16] The advice to seek after wisdom as a legitimate bride, moreover, stands in sharp contrast to the father's warning against the so-called strange or foreign woman elsewhere in Proverbs 1–9. The foreign woman is not described as a legitimate wife, but rather as an adulteress (or prostitute) whom the son finds sexually attractive. Just as Woman Wisdom is described as a legitimate bride and symbolically represents the right way, so the strange woman represents the often desirable but wrong way of folly and wickedness. In fact, the strange woman is symbolically identified with Woman Wisdom's opposite, Woman Folly, in Proverbs 9:13–18.

¹³The foolish woman is loud; she is ignorant and knows
nothing.

¹⁴She sits at the door of her house, on a seat at the high
places of the town,

¹⁵calling to those who pass by, who are going straight on
their way,

¹⁶"You who are simple, turn in here!" And to those without
sense she says,

¹⁷"Stolen water is sweet, and bread eaten in secret is
pleasant."

¹⁸But they do not know that the dead are there, that her
guests are in the depths of Sheol.

In chapter 4 the sages are again attempting to redirect readers'
attention from the pursuit of money, where some of us believe our
best opportunity for happiness and a fulfilled life lies, to the way of
wisdom, which is even more valuable than wealth. They intensify their
call by speaking of the desirability of wisdom in subtly erotic terms.

The sages are not asking us to forsake all our economic pur-
suits, for they knew that work and the quest for gain need not be
motivated solely by greed and could be directed toward good. John
Wesley, the eighteenth-century English founder of Methodism
(which became the United Methodist Church) promoted the maxim,
"Earn all you can, save all you can, give all you can." The goal was
not self-enrichment, but rather an ability to pursue (and finance)
causes for the greater good, such as (in Wesley's case) the pressing
need for social reforms, including prison reform and abolitionism.[17]
In our own day, organizations such as Goodwill Industries and the
Salvation Army use their thrift stores as an economic arm to help
achieve their larger purposes of combating poverty, addiction, and
other social ills.

Again, we might wonder what would happen if all the efforts and energies we spend on economic gain and seeking personal pleasures were turned toward acquiring the central virtues of wisdom's way, such as social justice. Our world would certainly look quite different.

"Take My Instruction, Not Silver!"—Proverbs 8:1–11

In Proverbs 8:1–11, the sages infuse the language of wisdom and money with a fresh sense of urgency. Yet here it is no longer simply the father or teacher who is speaking to the son. Rather, the sages of Proverbs have the voice of personified Wisdom teach us. After recounting in 8:1–3 how wisdom calls out to humans, the sages in 8:4–9 have her recite the noble acts she carries out:

> ¹Does not wisdom call, and does not understanding raise
> her voice?
> ²On the heights, beside the way, at the crossroads she takes
> her stand;
> ³beside the gates in front of the town, at the entrance of the
> portals she cries out:
> ⁴"To you, O people, I call, and my cry is to all that live.
> ⁵O simple ones, learn prudence; acquire intelligence, you
> who lack it.
> ⁶Hear, for I will speak noble things, and from my lips will
> come what is right;
> ⁷for my mouth will utter truth; wickedness is an abomina-
> tion to my lips.
> ⁸All the words of my mouth are righteous; there is nothing
> twisted or crooked in them.
> ⁹They are all straight to one who understands and right to
> those who find knowledge."

Then in 8:10–11 she continues:

> [10]Take my instruction instead of silver, and knowledge
> rather than choice gold,
> [11]for wisdom is better than jewels and all that you may
> desire cannot compare with her. (NRSV)

Verse 11 reminds us, as did Proverbs 3:14–15 (see p. 40), that wisdom is "better than," more valuable than, jewels and any material good or any amount of money we might desire. The Hebrew of at least the first half of verse 10, however, is a little more forceful than the above translation suggests. Rather than saying "Take my instruction instead of silver" it actually says something more like, "Take my instruction, not silver!"

Here we are a long way from the robbers' promise of "precious wealth" to those who would follow their way. In these lines the sages offer a more radical devaluation of all material wealth in relation to wisdom and her instruction than we have seen up to this point. According to the sages, we should grab on to wisdom and knowledge and *not* silver or gold. The value of wisdom and virtue is so great that we shouldn't bother at all pursuing material goods! St. Francis of Assisi, who was born to a wealthy merchant family in Italy in the late twelfth century and who abandoned his prosperous life for a life of poverty in service to the poor, is reported to have likewise commented that "We should have no more use or regard for money in any of its forms than we have for dust."[18]

Only Wisdom Endures—Proverbs 8:18–21

The last, and perhaps the most important, mention of money or material wealth in the first major section of the Book of Proverbs, chapters 1–9, occurs in Proverbs 8:18–21.

¹⁸Riches and honor are with me, enduring wealth and
  prosperity.
¹⁹My fruit is better than gold, even fine gold, and my yield
  than choice silver,
²⁰I walk in the way of righteousness, and along the paths of
  justice,
²¹Endowing with wealth those who love me and filling
  their treasuries. (NRSV)

There is much that is familiar in these lines. It is clear, for instance, from the first-person pronouns (*me, my, I*) that rather than the father or teacher speaking, it is personified Wisdom's words that we hear, as in 8:10–11. Verse 19, with its claims that wisdom is better than gold and silver is also reminiscent of 3:14–15 (see p. 40). Likewise verse 18, which associates "riches" and "honor" with wisdom, echoes 3:16 (see p. 40).

Verse 18 marks the high point, or pinnacle, of the redefining of money's worth in relation to wisdom's value that we have thus far been tracing in Proverbs. Yet how is this so, since at first glance the verse appears to represent a simple continuation of the process we have been considering? Indeed, just as earlier verses have associated images of money and wealth with wisdom in order to teach us that wisdom and virtue are more valuable than even riches, so does 8:18. But there are two important differences about verse 18 that make this line so very important for understanding what the sages of Proverbs are really up to when they talk so much about money and the way of wisdom.

First, in the previous verses where the sages talked about material wealth and wisdom's value, they used words that were different from the words the robbers used in chapter 1 to talk about the desirability of their way, the way of folly and wickedness. The robbers promised the son "precious wealth" (*hon yaqar*). Ever since that point the sages have been talking about wisdom's worth in terms of silver, gold, jewels, and so on, but not "wealth" or *hon*.[19] Here, however, the sages reintroduce the term *hon*. Yet rather than talk about *hon yaqar* or "precious wealth," Woman Wisdom says that she holds *hon 'ateq,* or "enduring wealth."

The Hebrew phrase *hon 'ateq* in 8:18 echoes the phrase *hon yaqar* in 1:13 (see p. 28). Whereas the robbers offered those who would follow their way the kind of wealth that possesses value in the economic realm, the sages have consistently implied that this sort of wealth has only a limited value. It is "precious" in the marketplace, perhaps, but it is not enduring or long lasting, like the kind of wealth that wisdom offers.

Indeed we can trace a progression in the sages' teaching about wisdom and wealth over the first eight chapters of Proverbs. After we learned about the sinners' promise of "precious wealth," we noted first in Proverbs 2 that we should seek wisdom *as* some of us might seek silver and treasures. Next, in Proverbs 3, we learned that wisdom possesses a value *greater than* that of material goods. In Proverbs 4 the sages instruct us to use whatever money or riches we might have to buy valuable wisdom. In Proverbs 8:10–11 (see p. 47) personified wisdom herself demanded that we take hold of her teaching "and not silver." Now in 8:18 we learn that what Woman Wisdom, the poetic or figurative personification of divine wisdom, holds and promises us is not primarily any real or literal material gain like that held out by the robbers in chapter 1. What wisdom holds is qualitatively different. She offers not "precious" material riches, but "enduring" or genuine wealth—wisdom and virtue.

But if wisdom is qualitatively more valuable than "precious wealth" because it is "enduring wealth," what precisely does this wisdom consist of? As the Prologue already tells us, it is a way of life that values, internalizes, and acts on intellectual and practical virtues, but especially the social virtues of justice, righteousness, and equity. Although Proverbs will later highlight a range of specific virtues that belong to wisdom's way in the sayings of chapters 10–29, verse 18 also offers a striking confirmation of the fact that the sages preeminently valued social virtue.

Most translations of the final word of verse 18 suggest that what wisdom holds is not only the "riches" and "honor" of the first half of the verse, or merely the "enduring wealth" that we just discussed, but also "prosperity" (NIV, NRSV) or "success" (JPS). This sort of language, however, might lead us to believe that what wisdom offers is material prosperity and that perhaps the "enduring wealth" of wisdom is, after all, best regarded more literally as real riches. However, the term in 8:18 that is regularly translated as "prosperity" or "success" is in Hebrew *tzedekah*—a word that is almost always rendered in the Bible as "righteousness" or "justice." It is closely related to those terms of social justice—*justice, righteousness, and equity (tzedek, mishpat,* and *meysharim*)—that were introduced to us way back in 1:3 of the Prologue (see p. 23). *Tzedekah* is even an etymological sibling to the term *tzedek,* which also is usually translated as "righteousness" or "justice."

Most likely, the term *tzedekah* is translated as "prosperity" or "success" in 8:18 (see p. 48) because, as we noted earlier, translators and interpreters generally assume that the book is largely about how wisdom promises financial success. Indeed, if the book is primarily about how we can achieve prosperity, then the concepts of righteousness or justice simply don't fit in 8:18 and one needs to find some other meaning for a word that is otherwise well known. But if the book is largely about social justice, as the Prologue suggests, and if verse 18's allusion to "enduring wealth" is a figurative allusion to that most valuable thing that wisdom holds, then encountering "justice" in this line makes perfect sense. Wisdom's value is the enduring or true value of virtue, especially social virtue.[20] Indeed, as Proverbs 8 continues we learn in verses 20–21 that personified wisdom herself travels the path of social justice.

> [20]I walk in the way of righteousness, along the paths of
>   justice,
> [21]endowing with wealth those who love me, and filling
>   their treasuries.

The fact that Proverbs 8:21 in most translations likewise speaks of wisdom's "wealth" (*yesh*) does not detract from our broader understanding of the passage, but rather underscores it. This is because the rendering of *yesh* as "wealth" is just as curious as the translation of *tzedekah* as "prosperity." In the Bible, *yesh* normally refers to "existence" and is most often translated as "there is." As with *tzedekah* in verse 18 (see p. 48), the decision to render *yesh* as "wealth" in verse 21 apparently rests largely on a preconceived understanding that the wisdom of Proverbs essentially constitutes a guide to material success. However, although what wisdom offers us is something very valuable, it is not primarily literal material riches. So, in light of the base meaning of *yesh*, what we know about the sages' inclination for tropes and figures, and especially given what we have thus far learned about the symbolic nature of wisdom's "wealth," it is best to understand the *yesh* that wisdom offers those who love her in 8:21 not as "wealth" but rather as something like genuine or true "existence."

According to the sages of Proverbs, then, to seek well-being or personal fulfillment in an inordinate pursuit of money or riches, and through all that money can buy, is wrongheaded. The frenzied pursuit and acquisition of more and more riches can never truly produce well-being or fulfillment. In fact, as we noted above, through stress, illness, and alienation from friends and family, the quest for more and more can actually be detrimental to achieving peace of mind and a flourishing life—and we cannot put a dollar figure on these sorts of intangible goods. They are not for sale. According to the sages of Proverbs, however, access to the kind of fulfilling existence many of us seek is to be found in wisdom and through the acquisition of wisdom's virtues.

Preeminent among the nonmaterial goods or character traits that the Book of Proverbs highlights is social virtue—a concern not merely for our own happiness and well-being, but for the well-being of everyone who makes up our communities. In the Bible, moreover, social justice—*mishpat* and *tzedekah*—is primarily a concern for the well-being of the poor and marginalized. It is a kind of solidarity with the disadvantaged of our world and the poor in our communities. It is a solidarity that, according to Latin American theologian Jon Sobrino, "means *letting oneself be affected* by the suffering of other human beings."[21] As we shall see below, beginning in Proverbs 10, the sages not only continue to underscore the value of wisdom, but flesh out more precisely what social virtue entails, and name many of the other virtues of wisdom's way. According to the sages, these virtues, which demand much of our personal and public lives, are in tune with the true moral nature of the cosmos, which is grounded in wisdom.

CHAPTER 3

Wisdom's Virtues in the Book of Proverbs

Up to this point, as we focused on the long wisdom poems of chapters 1–9, we have seen that the Book of Proverbs talks about how valuable the way of wisdom and virtue is. Using figurative language and metaphors, especially images of material wealth, the sages teach us that the way of wisdom and virtue is more valuable than riches: It is "enduring wealth." The path of wisdom, which is built into the very structure of creation, is where full and meaningful existence is to be found.

Now we turn to the short, artful sayings in the book's central nineteen chapters—those gems we usually think of as "proverbs." What do they have to say about money and the way of wisdom and virtue? Do these sayings offer the same, or a different, kind of message about the ultimate value of virtue over material wealth? How do they add to or expand on what the sages have said so far, and what impact does their message have for us today?

Wisdom, Virtue, and the "Proverbs" of Proverbs: Chapters 10–29

To answer these questions we need to recall that, in everyday life, proverbs derive their meaning from the moments and places in which they are spoken. But the sayings in the Book of Proverbs don't have a real-life context; they make up a collection and form part of a book. Hence, in a sense, they are dead. Yet as we indicated earlier, even these sayings can be given new life because they, too, have a context— a literary context. Just as we can understand spoken proverbs by paying attention to when and where they are used, so, too, we can get at the more specific meanings of the "proverbs" of Proverbs by paying attention to how they work in the broader literary context of the book—specifically, the context that has been established by the Prologue and the careful use of language in chapters 1–9. In this way we can continue to discern what the ancient sages wanted to teach us about money and wisdom through Proverbs.

Throughout the collections of short sayings in Proverbs 10–29, the sages reiterate their leading idea from Proverbs 1–9 regarding the incomparable value of wisdom's virtues, and do so by continuing to ascribe "worth" to wisdom by means of the language of material wealth. But now the virtues that are described are not merely the broad, *general* metavirtues of intellectual virtue, practical virtue, and social virtue. Rather, the sages begin to value by means of wealth and poverty language a range of *particular* values and virtues—such as love, humility, and peace—that together (and with other virtues) make up the whole of Proverbs' understanding of what wisdom comprises.

These sorts of wealth and poverty sayings help us see the specific contours of wisdom's path. They introduce us to the full range and context of Proverbs' moral teaching about money and riches, which can guide our lives today, as we ponder, for example, according to what criteria we might invest our money. (Should maximum return be our chief priority? What social or environmental considerations should we take into account?) As we shall see, however, the proverbs that transmit the particular virtues that make up wisdom's way are also intimately related to much of the sages' earlier teaching. In some ways they are specific instances of the intellectual, practical, and especially social virtues the sages highlighted at the beginning of Proverbs.

Similarities to Proverbs 1–9

Many of the proverbs in the later chapters of the Book of Proverbs recall and extend the basic ideas and literary strategies established by the Prologue and the long poems of chapters 1–9. This is accomplished in several ways.

Most obviously, a few sayings in the second half of Proverbs are reminiscent of the *language* of certain lines in the poems of chapters 1–9. Proverbs 16:16, for instance, says:

> Buy wisdom. So much better is it than gold. The acquisition
> of understanding is preferable to silver.

Proverbs 23:23 trades on the same marketplace metaphor of buying and selling wisdom when it says:

> Buy truth; and do not sell wisdom or instruction or
> understanding.

Both verses sound similar to Proverbs 4:7 (see p. 43), and, like several of the poems in chapters 1–9, these sayings use the language of money, buying, and selling to teach us how much more valuable wisdom and virtue are than any material goods.

A number of other short sayings in the second half of Proverbs, which employ wealth and poverty language, likewise resonate with the message of Proverbs 1–9.

> The wage of a righteous person leads to life; the produce
> of a wicked person to sin. (Proverbs 10:16)

The wicked earn an illusory wage, but the one who sows
righteousness has a true reward. (Proverbs 11:18)

The house of a righteous person is an abundant treasure;
but in the produce of a wicked person is something putrid.
(Proverbs 15:6)

The contrast between the righteous and the wicked person in these
verses recalls that fundamental moral distinction between the "two
ways" that was so clear in chapters 1–9, especially in Proverbs 1,
where the robbing and murdering sinners represented one way that
leads to death and the words of the father or teacher pointed to the
other, which leads to life. As in Proverbs 1–9, in these sayings the
sages also ascribe value or worth to each of the two ways by using
the language of economics. The righteous or just person and the
wicked person are each said to receive a "wage" or "reward." They
can expect their way of life to result in a particular payoff or
"produce" in the subtle agricultural metaphor underlying all three
proverbs.

Notice, for instance, that in 10:16 the wicked person's "produce" or "wage"—what he gains from his way of life—is associated
with sin. Similarly in chapter 1 the robbers are called "sinners,"
which in Hebrew suggests fundamentally that they have somehow
missed the mark of the kind of life that the sages endorse. They have
refused to put themselves on the right side of the moral cosmos, to
align themselves with wisdom's way. Although the robbers promise
that their way will produce valuable wealth, the father insists that
it leads to death. Analogously Proverbs 11:18 speaks of the wicked
person's "reward" as something "illusory," and Proverbs 15:6,
although the Hebrew is difficult, might even suggest that it is something that is decaying or "putrid"—a way that is rotting. Although

those on the wrong path in the above proverbs can expect a reward—and the images here indicate that their economic activities might result in a material reward or money—the sages poetically insist that, like the sinners of Proverbs 1, they will not ultimately end well. Their "reward" is of no lasting value.

This ancient and vivid language might be used to describe events in our own day. The "illusory wage" that the wicked earn recalls the scandal involving the Enron Corporation, which erupted in 2001 when the Texas-based energy company's accounting practices were discovered to be deeply fraudulent. In subsequent investigations and trials, the company was found to be riddled with corruption, motivated by a shocking level of greed that reached to the very top of Enron's management. The company collapsed, and within months, what had been one of Wall Street's top-trading energy stocks was all but worthless.[1]

By contrast, the wage or reward of the virtuous person in the above proverbs, the person who is characterized by righteousness and justice—or social virtue—is called "life" (10:16) and is described as "true" (11:18) and as "abundant treasure" (15:6). Although especially this last turn of phrase (*abundant treasure*) in 15:6 might suggest to some that the virtuous can expect a material reward, the term translated as "treasure" is rather general and is not one of the usual terms the sages use to talk about material riches, wealth, or money. This suggests that here, like the "life" and "true reward" of 10:16 and 11:18, the promise to those who follow wisdom's way is not primarily one of literal wealth, but of the figurative riches of genuine well-being and fulfillment in life. Hence, just as the sayings poetically reiterate some of the main claims of Proverbs 1 about the true, dismal end, or "reward," of those who strive for wealth via the way of folly, so, too, the sayings underscore the sages' earlier teaching regarding the genuine, but not merely material, recompense of those who seek wisdom. Their reward is not simply or primarily money and riches, but the "enduring wealth" (see Proverbs 8:18, p. 48) that wisdom's virtues confer.

Besides the use of familiar economic language to describe the value of wisdom's way, the above-cited verses also call to mind a further similarity to the sages' teaching in Proverbs 1–9, especially in chapter 1, namely the wise instruction that calls us to reject the pursuit and acquisition of money and material riches by unjust means. This important message, along with the corollary that the possession of money and wealth can't be taken uncritically as a sign of divine favor or moral uprightness—and may be a sign of wickedness and injustice—is reiterated in other short sayings in the second half of Proverbs as well.

> Treasures of wickedness do not profit, but righteousness
> rescues from death. (Proverbs 10:2)

> Whoever pursues unjust gain makes trouble for his house;
> whoever hates a bribe will live. (Proverbs 15:27)

> Treasures gained by a tongue of deception are a driven mist,
> seekers of death. (Proverbs 21:6)

As in Proverbs 1 each of these sayings asserts that money gained by unsavory means is ultimately not valuable, as far as the sages are concerned. Such economic advantage does not "profit" (10:2); it "makes trouble" (15:27) and is "deception" (21:6). It is a "mist" (21:6), a term that the Book of Ecclesiastes uses repeatedly to describe the meaninglessness and lack of any ultimate value in life. This last verse (21:6) is especially difficult in Hebrew, but may suggest, as did the teacher in Proverbs 1, that those who pursue unjust gain end up with something that lacks value, and actually pursue their own death. By contrast, Proverbs 15:27, which employs a rhetoric of unjust gain that precisely echoes that of Proverbs 1, also notes that those who avoid such economic quests for advantage will live. This line also notes an example of an unjust economic practice that should be rejected—namely, bribery—a proverbial topic we will explore more fully in chapter 4.

To our ears today, however, all this talk about the wicked and unjust not profiting from their evil deeds might sound somewhat naïve. Many of us know that all too often those who gain their wealth through specious means do enjoy it for a long time. The sages, too, certainly understood that those who acquired money and riches unjustly could, and often did, benefit financially from their gains. However, the sages' concern is not primarily with whether some, or even many, wicked people *actually* derive some economic advantage from their unjustly gained riches. In uttering their proverbs they are not so much interested in whether certain unscrupulous people in fact enjoy some real net increase in possessions or power, or if some of the Enrons of the world go unexposed and unpunished. The sages were not social scientists looking for empirical evidence to confirm the "facts" of their poetry. Rather, they were interested in larger matters of truth. These proverbs help us distinguish money and material gain from what is of genuine value; they also help us discern what virtues and character traits we can acquire that will bring true and enduring life and fulfillment. The sages wanted to help us see how worthwhile it is for us to adopt wisdom's virtues and to align our lives and morality with what they believed is the genuine structure of the cosmos, which was created "in wisdom." Or in Dr. Martin Luther King Jr.'s idiom, they invite us to identify and then trace with our lives the moral arc of the universe that bends toward justice (see note 7 in the Introduction).

Had the sages been able to see into our own day, they might have viewed the recent trend toward "socially responsible investing" as one way the moral arc of the universe can help orient our day-to-day financial decisions, as one step down the path of wisdom. Although specifics vary, those who practice socially responsible investing, which today accounts for about one in every ten dollars invested,[2] seek to invest only in companies or funds that meet certain ethical, environmental, or humanitarian criteria—for example, mutual funds that refuse to include in their portfolio tobacco companies or weapons manufacturers. In the argot of the sages, this might be thought of as "socially virtuous investing."

Prosperity versus the "Good Life"

Several other proverbs in Proverbs 10–29 also reflect the same fundamental perspective the sages articulate in Proverbs 1–9; namely, that the reward of the one who follows wisdom's way will not be mere material prosperity, but a broader experience of a good and contented life. However, in English translation this point can sometimes be lost. Consider the following sayings as rendered by the NRSV.

> Misfortune pursues sinners, but *prosperity* rewards the righteous. (Proverbs 13:21)

> Those who are attentive to a matter will *prosper,* and happy are those who trust in the Lord. (Proverbs 16:20)

> To get wisdom is to love oneself; to keep understanding is to *prosper.* (Proverbs 19:8) [Emphasis mine]

In each of these lines, the language of prospering and prosperity, which I have italicized for emphasis, suggests that those who follow wisdom's way of righteousness will find some material blessing. However, in each verse behind the rhetoric of prospering lies the Hebrew term *tov*, which refers to something "good" or "pleasing," and hence to one's "welfare" or "well-being" or "happiness." Although *tov* can carry the sense of "prosperity," the NRSV's rendering of the Hebrew this way again reflects that tendency among scholars and translators to understand Proverbs as a book that in relatively straightforward ways promises material success to the one who pursues wisdom. However, in these lines the sages do not explicitly promise riches, money, wealth, or any material gain. So we should understand the "good" that is promised in these lines as a full and flourishing life. It is a life that brings not merely material gain, but also a more fundamental happiness, contentment, and peace, free from the temptation that wealth itself, even if honestly gained, can pose. Indeed as 16:20 explicitly states, those who walk the way of wisdom by trusting in the divine are "happy." These people have accepted the sages' vision and have begun to align their lives with the wisdom that infuses the cosmos.

Expanding on Proverbs 1–9

Looking closely at the proverbs of Proverbs 10–29, we discover that much as the narrative poems in chapters 1–9 expand on the basic purpose sketched in the Prologue, these short, well-crafted sayings also extend the range and scope of the sages' teaching about wisdom and wealth.

For instance, if we were reading some of the proverbs we just examined in isolation (say, Proverbs 10:2; 15:27; or 21:6—see p. 58), it might be easy to claim that the sages were decrying only the *unjust* pursuit of money and economic gain as something inherently wicked, but not disparaging money itself or its *legitimate* pursuit in any way. Many scholars make this point, and such proverbs do reveal the sages' clear disdain for economic injustice. Dr. King once said, "Money, like any other force, such as electricity, is amoral and can be used for either good or evil."[3] We would, however, be incorrect if we assumed that the sages were only exhorting us to avoid the evils of *unjust gain,* and were not also warning us about the dangers of money and its pursuit more generally. Consider, for instance, Proverbs 11:4 and 11:28:

> Wealth does not profit on the day of wrath, but righteousness rescues from death. (Proverbs 11:4)

> Whoever trusts in riches will fall, but the righteous will burst forth like a leaf. (Proverbs 11:28)

Unlike some of the sayings we studied above, these proverbs do not mention any sort of "unjust gain," only riches, unmodified by any negative-sounding adjective. Proverbs 11:4 claims simply that wealth does not profit, at least not in certain circumstances—namely, the "day of wrath." Some scholars claim that the day of wrath may refer to a day of divine judgment. If so, it is an image that belongs to the religious and moral realm. The sages' point is not that wealth does not profit in the marketplace, its proper realm, if you will. Their point is that it has no currency outside that realm—or at least it ought not to.

Some scholars assert that the wealth mentioned in 11:4 must refer to "ill-gotten wealth." However, the text does not say this. Moreover, to insist that the line must have this sense—a view probably based on the common way of understanding the Book of Proverbs as a straight forward guide to material prosperity—is to miss an important point of the instruction. If Proverbs does constitute a guide to prosperity, it wouldn't make sense for the sages to limit the value of riches unless they were unjustly gained.

Most scholars note that the problem in 11:4 and 11:28 is not with money or wealth itself, but with "trusting" in it. This sort of statement attempts to underscore the neutrality of wealth. It only becomes a problem when we overvalue it.

What is missing in this sort of analysis is an understanding of how the sages here move their instruction to a new level by recognizing and warning us against the danger that the unfettered pursuit and accumulation of *any sort of wealth* poses to the way of wisdom. The sages teach us not merely that the pursuit of wealth can be undertaken wickedly and become the pursuit of unjust gain. They also lay bare for us a human shortcoming—namely, that many of us often overvalue wealth, hoping that it will provide us with the good life we seek. In addition, the sages hint that the pursuit and possession of wealth is fundamentally risky, precisely because it is so valuable and desirable and so often appears to hold the key to contentment. Few among us who have acquired much wealth can completely withstand the temptation to "trust" in it, or in the social and political power that it confers. Greed and arrogance are the threats to character that follow if, like the robbers in Proverbs 1, we cannot find a way to align ourselves with a moral vision strong enough to counter this tendency.

We have seen that Proverbs' moral teaching about wealth is much more than a road map to success. The sages' claim here is thus better understood as part of their larger project of redescribing for us—this time in terms of even *justly* gained wealth—what is of greatest value in life. Although some of us mistakenly place our faith primarily in money and riches—a lucrative career, an aggressive investment portfolio, and so on—these ultimately cannot deliver the life we are seeking. Rabbi Irving Greenberg notes that the quest for wealth can help "free people from poverty" and enable them "to lead lives of greater dignity"; nevertheless, he emphasizes, "Increased wealth alone is not redemptive, particularly if it is not distributed widely."[4] Indeed, according to Proverbs 11:4, only justice or right-eousness, the kind of social justice the Prologue highlighted and to which Rabbi Greenberg alludes, can save us "from death."

The second of the two sayings cited above, 11:28, sharply diagnoses the very trap that some of us fall into; namely, believing or expecting that our money and material well-being, legitimate or not, will lead to the contentment for which our spirits long. "Those who trust in their riches," says 11:28, "will fall." By contrast, "The righteous," those who follow wisdom's way and pursue its virtues, "will burst forth like a leaf." The image of budding vegetation aptly captures what is at stake for the sages. Without denying money's value in certain spheres of life or the virtue of hard work—both of which might be harnessed for the good of others to create the material conditions we all need so that our whole beings might flourish—the sages proclaim that the genuine life that many of us seek is not to be found primarily in the pursuit of dollars and the merchandise it can buy.

One well-known ancient Jewish sage, Jesus ben Sira (Sirach), once noted that it was nearly impossible for the merchants of his day (much like modern-day, overly driven businesspeople) "to keep from wrongdoing" or "to be declared innocent of sin" (Sirach 26:29). Sirach most likely did not mean for his somewhat exaggerated words to serve as a blanket condemnation of all who pursue business. But he certainly meant to make us stop and think about how our pursuit of more and more money can lead us down the wrong path. Another even more famous ancient Jewish sage also named Jesus—Jesus of Nazareth—similarly claimed that it is easier for a "rich person to pass through the eye of a needle" than to enter into the just "kingdom of God," about which he preached (Matthew 19:24). He also claimed that "you cannot serve God and wealth" (Matthew 6:24). The way of pursuing wealth, Jesus claimed, was opposed to the way of serving the Divine, which the sages of Proverbs surely would have understood as the way of wisdom. Like Jesus, the sages of Proverbs recognized that the pursuit and possession of money and wealth by *whatever* means undermines the life of wisdom, precisely because riches are so desirable. As still another ancient Jewish sage associated with the Book of Ecclesiastes, Kohelet, put it,

> The lover of money will not be satisfied with money, nor the lover of gain with wealth. (Ecclesiastes 5:10)

A modern Jewish wise man, Albert Einstein, reiterated the view of his forebears when he likewise claimed to be "absolutely convinced that no amount of wealth can help humanity forward, even in the hands of the most dedicated worker in this cause" because "Money only appeals to selfishness, and, without fail it tempts its owner to abuse it."[5]

Proverbs' Particular Virtues

If a number of the sayings in the second half of Proverbs communicate a message quite similar to the message of the first half of the book, many other proverbs that speak about wealth and poverty have messages distinct from those in the poems in Proverbs 1–9. In this second half, the sages give us more concrete instruction about precisely what facets of the way of wisdom are valuable, what virtues are of great worth. As we shall see, all these virtues are related to the sages' overall message, especially their emphasis on social virtue. For the sages, a full, rewarding existence primarily stems from the pursuit and acquisition of character traits that contribute to communal well-being, not the pursuit of individual wealth.

Right Speech

Several sayings in Proverbs 10–29 teach us about the importance or value of the words we use in conversing with one another—how we speak as we walk the way of wisdom.

> The tongue of the righteous person is choice silver, but the mind of the wicked is like something of little worth. (Proverbs 10:20)

> There is gold, and abundance of costly stones, but lips of knowledge are a precious vessel. (Proverbs 20:15)

> Golden apples in a silver showpiece is a phrase well turned; a ring of gold, a golden ornament, is a wise person's reproof in a receptive ear. (Proverbs 25:11–12)

Eloquent and inspiring words, certainly. Nevertheless, as we ponder how these sorts of proverbs can be adapted for use in our own lives, we quickly find ourselves confronted with the question of context that we explored in chapter 1. In short, we don't know exactly how they were used in some ancient oral context or the meaning they would have carried then. Although we may want to venture a guess at some context, or even be open to new real-life situations where we might "recontextualize" these sorts of sayings, the only reliable context that we have for understanding them is the literary context of the Book of Proverbs. Indeed, their complex structure suggests that they are the final products of scribes who were composing literature and not simple, oral proverbs that can be taken literally.

When considering a saying like 10:20, for instance, we can easily recognize that the righteous or just person's tongue is not literally made of silver. Yet remembering that throughout their book the sages of Proverbs regularly use tropes and figures to teach us about virtue, we will immediately understand that such a person's tongue forms words that are of great worth. Similarly "lips of knowledge" (20:15) and a wise reproof (25:12)—what we might call *right speech*—are as valuable as precious material goods: gold, silver, costly stones.

That a person's tongue is literally not made of metal may be obvious. But what exactly is the right speech that these proverbs claim *is* so valuable? The broader literary context of the proverbs gives us our first clues. Proverbs 25:11's talk of "a phrase well turned" and 20:15's mention of "lips of knowledge" suggest that the sages on one level are talking about the practical virtue (cf. 1:4, p. 23) of being able to speak well and communicate one's point to another. We may imagine a respected teacher or mentor guiding a pupil along the paths of life with her lectures and words of insight. Indeed the sages' concern with right speech is widespread in Proverbs.[6] But Proverbs 25:12 also speaks of "reproof," which carries a stronger moral connotation, as does the mention in 10:20 of the "righteous" or just person's speech.

This sort of rhetoric hints to us that the right speech that we can adopt as we traverse wisdom's path is related to justice and the kind of social virtue that the Prologue highlighted as particularly important. On the one hand, the "just person" in Hebrew is the *tzadik*, a term that must, in part, mean that the tongue of this person promotes social justice—the *tzedek* or *tzedekah* that Proverbs elsewhere values so highly. On the other hand, reproof is nothing other than sound correction. When it is rightly offered to other people, however, it also carries a social dimension. Again, the image of a teacher comes to mind, correcting a student, when necessary. Likewise, sound correction by the person of virtue helps to keep not only individuals, but also groups of people and communities on the path of wisdom.

Think, for instance, of the public reproaches offered by ancient Israel's prophets. Amos decried those who "sell the righteous for silver and the needy for a pair of sandals" and who "trample the head of the poor into the dust of the earth" (Amos 2:6–7). Jeremiah dared to challenge the social injustice he saw around him (Jeremiah 22), spoke out against the "foreign policy" of his king, and was imprisoned and thrown into a muddy cistern for doing so (Jeremiah 37–38), having earlier been threatened with death for his prophetic sermons (Jeremiah 26). In our own era, Dr. Martin Luther King Jr. used scathing terms to publicly rebuke the perpetrators of injustice and racism. Not surprisingly, many in Amos's, Jeremiah's, and King's times were offended and enraged by their public statements. Even J. Edgar Hoover, then the head of the FBI, once called Dr. King "the most notorious liar in the country" because of his public denunciations of racism, war, and poverty—though Dr. King was perhaps the greatest truth teller the United States has ever known.[7] Before he was ultimately assassinated, Dr. King, like Jeremiah, was imprisoned and threatened with death.

Nevertheless, Dr. King's words, aligned as they were with the moral arc of the universe, also contained the power to inspire and enlighten. His tongue, you might say, was of "choice silver," inasmuch as it promoted justice. So, too, we can practice "right speech," promoting justice when necessary and issuing rebukes in order to guide others along the path of wisdom. This is so whether we are called to be among those who utter wise and valuable admonishments, or among those exhorted by contemporary prophets to return to wisdom's way of justice.

Building Community through Love, Humility, and Peace

Not only do the proverbs of Proverbs expand on the teaching of Proverbs 1–9 by using images of material well-being to talk about the value of particular virtues like "right speech," they also advance the teaching of the book's initial poems in at least two other ways. First, the sages in the second half of the book not only use images of material riches to speak of the worth of virtue, they use images of material poverty to talk about the lack of value of certain vices. (We actually have already seen an example of this in Proverbs 10:20 [see p. 66], which spoke not only of a just person's tongue being like silver, but of a wicked person's mind being like "something of little worth.") Second, the sages extend the repertoire of rhetorical techniques through which they teach us about wisdom and money.

One typical and powerful way the sages in Proverbs 10–29 use wealth and poverty language to talk about the value of the virtues of wisdom's way (and likewise the lack of worth of certain vices) is by using what scholars have termed "better than" sayings—sayings that announce that one thing is better than, or of more worth than, something else. Although not absent in Proverbs 1–9, this rhetorical device is more common in the book's later chapters. Proverbs 16:8 and 28:6 exemplify this method; they also use the language of wealth and poverty:

> Better a little with righteousness, than abundant produce without justice. (Proverbs 16:8)

> Better a poor person walking in his uprightness, than a person of perverse ways who is rich. (Proverbs 28:6)

In these sayings, the *virtues* ("uprightness") are associated with *negative* economic images ("poor person"). However, the logic of the sayings, which nonetheless value virtue over vice, is fairly easy to discern. The "better than" language is the key. In both lines the first half of the saying pairs a negative economic image with a moral positive or virtue, while the second half of the line pairs a moral negative or vice with a positive economic image. The sayings suggest that the former is better than the latter. The economic negative with the moral positive trumps the economic positive with the moral negative. Righteousness or justice—the way of wisdom—even if it is accompanied by material lack is better than injustice or another moral vice, even if one were to possess much money or great wealth. These two "better than" sayings artfully reiterate the great worth of the way of wisdom and righteousness, which was the basic orientation of Proverbs 1–9.

A host of other "better than" sayings that employ economic images reveal other specific virtues that the ancient sages deemed more valuable than money and material goods. These virtues again fill out for us a particular or concrete picture of wisdom's way. Proverbs 15:7, for instance, underscores the value of love over hate:

> Better a meal of vegetables where there is love than a fattened ox where there is hate.

Proverbs 16:19 highlights the worth of humility over undue pride:

> Better to be humble and among the poor than to divide the spoil with the proud.

Proverbs 17:1 recognizes the advantage of maintaining a peaceful household over one that is characterized by strife:

> Better a dry crust with peace than a house full of feasting with strife.

Each of these "better than" proverbs instructs us about the value of particular moral traits and follows a logic similar to those sayings we examined above. Even if accompanied by economic or material hardship, the virtues the proverbs tout are more valuable than the possession of great wealth sans such exemplary character.

These sorts of sayings challenge our tendency to judge people based on their economic standing rather than on the quality of their character. The sages remind us that there is no direct correspondence between the possession of virtue and the possession of money. But what is perhaps most important for us today is to notice that the different virtues of love, humility, and peace that these sayings promote are not unrelated to the sages' overall understanding of money and virtue and the worth of each. The virtues these proverbs promote are exactly the kinds of qualities that are necessary for building the social equity and harmony that the Prologue reminds us the ancient sages valued so highly. These virtues bolster social relations; without them (and other virtues) we cannot experience the security of community nor can we acknowledge the profound insight that German theologian Jürgen Moltmann has articulated: "The opposite of poverty isn't property. The opposite of both poverty and property is community. For in community we become rich: rich in friends, in neighbors, in colleagues, in comrades, in brothers and sisters."[8]

Avoiding the Vices of the Rich

A number of other proverbs in the Book of Proverbs use the language of money, or wealth and poverty, figuratively to value still other specific virtues and vices. In doing so, they help us see what kind of character they hoped to inculcate in their students.

A person of lack is the one who loves pleasure; whoever loves wine and oil will not gain riches. (Proverbs 21:17)

Do not be among those who guzzle wine or glut themselves on meat. For guzzlers and gluttons will be dispossessed, and drowsing will clothe you in tatters. (Proverbs 23:20–21)

These proverbs associate poverty or lack of riches with those who love pleasure, wine, oil, and meat. At first blush, it may appear that these sayings are simply concerned with offering instruction in a practical virtue—table manners. Some scholars suggest that the lines convey straightforward, no-nonsense advice that would have been especially useful for ancient scribes who may have found themselves dining in the presence of their social and political superiors.

However, by now we are well aware that even simple-sounding instruction in Proverbs often subtly masks a more profound point. When we look closely at the proverbs just cited, we see that they speak specifically of excessive consumption, of guzzling and gluttony, the "love of" pleasure, wine, and oil. They are not merely concerned with table manners. They also censure a profligate lifestyle, implicitly comparing it with one that is characterized by hard work and industry. In the ancient world, moreover, wine, oil, and meat were luxury goods and would have been consumed primarily by the economic elite. The sayings hence implicitly suggest that the vices they highlight are not just any old vices, but, specifically, if stereotypically, the vices of the rich. Like Proverbs 11:28 (see p. 62), which spoke of the "trust" some put in riches, these sayings also begin to locate threats to a life of wisdom in the world of wealth. The sages of Proverbs are saying that wealth has a tendency to transform those who possess it into people who are largely defined by what they have, and how insatiably they consume.

These sorts of sayings begin to cut close to home for those of us who regularly enjoy a good meal and a fine bottle of wine. In fact, people living in the United States consume more meat per capita than any other nation. According to a January 2008 *New York Times* article, U.S. citizens consume, on average, eight ounces of meat per day, roughly twice the global average. All totaled, the United States, which makes up about 5 percent of the world's population, consumes 15 percent of the world's meat.[9] Similarly, according to a January 2006 *San Francisco Chronicle* article, the per capita consumption of wine in the United States is at a record high as well.[10] But it is important to note that the sages are not simply condemning the eating of meat and the drinking of wine as something that is always and everywhere suspect. In fact, Kohelet, the sage of Ecclesiastes whom we mentioned earlier, recommends that we enjoy the food we have as a gift from God. Rather, through these proverbs the sages ask us to use our intellectual capacities to question our motives and to heighten our awareness about how we, too, might be profligate with our bounty. With Proverbs in mind, we need to reflect on the astonishing statistic, about who consumes what, with which we began this book: The richest fifth of the world's people consumes 86 percent of all goods and services while the poorest fifth consumes just 1.3 percent.

We have heard it before, but it is worth repeating that the United States is insatiable in its appetite for natural resources. A piece in the *New York Times,* titled "American Wastefulness," notes with colorful language that "Americans are playing the prodigal son with their inheritance. The immense resources of the country are wasted.... As a people, we are lavish beyond any other in our personal habits and ways of living.... It is rightly said that in the mere matter of eating and drinking, a Frenchman would live upon what an American wastes."[11]

These words certainly ring true to contemporary ears, but, surprisingly, this article was published in 1867! When it comes to curbing our profligate lifestyle, we have not made much progress in the last century and half.

The sages would surely not have viewed such thoughtless, self-centered behavior—whether in 1867 or today—as belonging to the way of wisdom. Their sayings point out that most of us in North America, as individuals and certainly as a society, are "rich." If we reflect seriously on the sages' words, we have to ask ourselves how profligate we are, how much we behave like guzzlers. The sages ask us to consider how, through our consumption, we seek some sense of security or well-being that keeps eluding us. They urge us to ponder whether or not we deploy our resources toward wisdom's ends of promoting social harmony. Many of us may be wealthy, but this does not mean that we have to be "rich" in the pejorative way the sages describe it. The challenge is to discover a way to live with our wealth that the sages would recognize as being in accord with a cosmos they believed was constructed by wisdom.

If Proverbs 21:17 (see p. 71) and 23:20–21 (see p. 72) censure excessive consumption, other verses in Proverbs deploy wealth and poverty language precisely to promote the virtue of generosity while not provoking the spirit of greed.

> ²⁴There is one who scatters and increases more; and one
>   who withholds what is right—only for lack.
> ²⁵A generous person will grow fat, and one who gives
>   water will also get water.
> ²⁶The one who withholds grain will be cursed by the
>   people, but blessing is for the head of the one who
>   dispenses it. (Proverbs 11:24–26)

Proverbs 11:24–26 paradoxically suggests that by giving what you have you can increase what you have. Again for the sages who skillfully employ tropes and figures to instruct us in virtue, the concern is not whether such sayings are literally always true or not. Their concern is not to teach us how to "get more." Here the sages are trying to motivate us to acquire and practice the virtue of generosity and to vanquish any greediness from our spirits. Greed runs against the grain of the moral cosmos, but generosity infuses a wise character, which corresponds to the stuff of creation. Much like John Wesley, mentioned earlier, the sages ask us to be wise stewards of what we have, to employ our resources in the service of others. As the theologian, musician, and physician Albert Schweitzer once remarked, "Life becomes harder for us when we live for others, but it also becomes richer and happier."[12]

The proverbs of Proverbs like those considered above ask us to learn that the way of virtue is a way that while seeking the social and economic well-being of others and not merely ourselves, actually can contribute to the peace of mind and security we seek. The sages ask us to recognize that looking to the betterment of others, which perhaps might cost us economically, results not merely in a good feeling, but can also help remove the animosity of others and so also diminish the anxiety, and sometimes even fear, we have of our neighbors around town and around the world. Recall again the words of Moltmann, "In community we become rich: rich in friends, in colleagues, in comrades, in brothers and sisters" (see note 8, this chapter).

The sages certainly would be pleased to learn that the generosity they promote can accord with our financial decisions, even in today's cut-throat corporate environment. For example, in 2000 Microsoft founder Bill Gates (along with his wife) launched the Bill and Melinda Gates Foundation, with two goals. In the United States, the foundation "seeks to ensure that all people—especially those with the fewest resources—have access to the opportunities they need to succeed in school and life." In developing nations, the foundation "focuses on improving people's health and giving them the chance to lift themselves out of hunger and extreme poverty." The foundation has given away more than $16 billion since its inception.[13] In 2006 stock market investment guru Warren Buffett gave the Gates foundation an unprecedented gift worth $31 million. Although the sages' sensibilities would surely make them suspicious of those, like the Gates and Buffett, who wield so much economic power, these donors' philanthropy resists any simplistic characterization of their and others' motivations.

In this regard, we should also note that one of the sayings cited above, Proverbs 11:26 (see p. 74), may be specifically addressed to and designed to influence the behavior of the economically privileged, as perhaps were Proverbs 21:17 (see p. 71) and 23:20–21 (see p. 72). The saying "The one who withholds grain will be cursed by the people, but blessing is for the head of the one who dispenses it" (11:26), of course, could be heard by anyone as generally promoting generosity. But its rhetoric of withholding and distributing grain echoes the story of Joseph, who in Genesis is said to have risen in rank until he controlled all the storehouses of Egypt. The sages thus probably understood such a saying as most pertinent to a politically or economically powerful figure—one who had the power to withhold or distribute the means of life, as Joseph did. Here, and as we will see more fully below, the sages suggest that those in privileged economic or political positions have particularly strong obligations to cultivate and act based on social virtue.

The sages' words present a moral dilemma to those of us who live in the richest countries of the world. Their words challenge not only individualistic thinking, but also the ideology of capitalism, the economic system predominant in our world, which claims that by seeking our own economic well-being we also promote the well-being of others. Adam Smith in *The Wealth of Nations* called this the work of the "invisible hand."[14] The sages' words lead us to ask if the rising economic tide of capitalism truly lifts all boats or whether it merely lifts our boats while inundating others. Joseph Stiglitz, the Nobel Laureate quoted earlier answers this question starkly: "It is not true that 'a rising tide lifts all boats.' Sometimes, a quickly rising tide, especially when accompanied by a storm, dashes weaker boats against the shore, smashing them to smithereens."[15]

This is not to uncritically decry free market capitalism. This system produces enormous wealth and has, in some cases, greatly diminished poverty. Yet we need to recognize that it primarily serves the interests of the most economically privileged, and is not, as George Soros has put it, "competent to ensure social justice"[16]—precisely the matters that the sages of Proverbs tell us ought to be our guide when thinking about our money.

Strident critics and supporters of the system alike must address the sages' demands that we use our intellectual and practical reasoning powers to consider how wisdom's virtues might be more fully realized in our lives and the world. Even those elements of the capitalist system that rightly come under attack may yield some good. (For all the possibly well-deserved criticism aimed at Wal-Mart in recent years, in 2006 it was America's leading corporate donor to charitable organizations, giving more than $270 million. This certainly complicates any evaluation of our remarkably complex economic systems.)[17]

Recognizing the inequities inherent in our capitalist economic arrangements, how will we repair or reform them? If we believe we need to scrap this system, what will take its place? And will the new system more fully guide us toward and be guided by wisdom's way? Are we willing to do the sort of hard work the authors of

Alternatives to Economic Globalization have done, inquiring about how our economies, our communal economic lives, might serve all and not just a few?[18] The sages of Proverbs insist we attend to the prophetic voices in our world that demand that we recognize how we as individuals and communities have strayed from wisdom's way. They also ask us to consider how we will go about finding a way to return to the right path. For the sages, the prophetic critique is only the beginning.

Laziness and Diligence

The sages of Proverbs took special care to address two specific items, one virtue and one vice, that they wanted readers to embrace and shun, respectively: *diligence* on the one hand, and *sloth,* or laziness, on the other. Given what we've discovered thus far, it is to be expected that the sages of Proverbs would use wealth and poverty language to encourage and exhort their audience, including us today, to become diligent and avoid laziness. This is exactly what they did. However, this sort of rhetorical strategy can and has produced much confusion.

The sayings about diligence and laziness that use images of material riches and economic lack can often sound like quasisociological observations about how rich and poor people come to exist. They have even been used at times to blame the poor for their poverty (castigating them as lazy good-for-nothings) and congratulate the rich for their supposed virtue. That is, these proverbs have sometimes been understood to support the prosperity gospel view of reality, which is a distortion of the sages' teaching. But to understand these sayings in this way is to miss the subtlety of their rhetoric and to fail to understand how they function in the overall moral system that the Book of Proverbs presents. Indeed as we said above, although various proverbs that are used by a particular community or society may offer perspectives that sound contradictory, these sayings might nonetheless actually form complementary components of a single, more complex moral system.

Consider, for example the following proverbs:

A slack hand makes a poor person, but the hand of the diligent enriches. (Proverbs 10:4)

The one who works his land will be sated with bread, but the one who pursues vanities has no sense. (Proverbs 12:11)

In all toil is profit, but mere talk makes only for lack. (Proverbs 14:23)

Do not love sleep lest you be impoverished; open your eyes, have plenty of bread. (Proverbs 20:13)[19]

When compared with other proverbs in Proverbs, which almost pedantically contrast the wise with the fool or the wicked with the righteous, these sayings sound more like the kind of folk proverbs many of us know or have read in modern collections of proverbs. They don't have the strong literary feel that some of the other sayings we have considered possess. When you remember that ancient Israelite society was based largely on peasant and subsistence agriculture, you might think that these sorts of sayings originally emerged from just such a context. When and where people live off the land, it is very important to promote hard work, and it is easy to imagine that someone who is lazy, and who loves sleep and vanities, will end up being poor.

Hence, it might be tempting for us to simply, or simplistically, accept the surface meaning of these proverbs or let a superficial reading of such sayings inform our own opinions about those who are less well off than we are. But if we did this, we would be missing a crucial aspect of the teaching these sayings can offer us.

As it turns out, a peasant agricultural context probably is not the best background against which to assess the lazy-diligent sayings of the Book of Proverbs. A peasant farmer in the ancient world would never have had sufficient leisure time or opportunity to learn to write and read difficult texts like Proverbs. By the same token, a scribe would never have had the time and energy requisite to engage in basic agriculture. So, once again, it is better to look to the literary context of Proverbs and to understand the lazy-diligent sayings in light of what we've already learned about how the book works.

Although the sages certainly didn't shy away from using wealth and poverty language to describe the relative value of diligence and laziness, it is vital to note that they also used other language to describe the relative worth of this virtue and this vice. This insight confirms that with the lazy-diligent sayings, the sages of Proverbs are concerned about promoting the value of the virtue of diligence itself, rather than teaching us how people become rich and poor.

Consider, for instance, Proverbs 10:26 and 15:19:

Like vinegar to the teeth and like smoke to the eyes, thus
is the lazy person to the one sending him. (Proverbs 10:26)

The way of the lazy person is like a hedge of thorns, but the
path of the upright is paved. (Proverbs 15:19)

Neither of these proverbs mentions anything about money or riches; neither discusses how you attain or lose wealth, depending on whether you are lazy or diligent. Rather, both associate laziness with something that is not pleasant or desirable: a sour taste in the mouth and smoke in the eyes, or a hedge of thorns that prevents you from continuing on your way. In Proverbs 15:19, the lazy person is compared to the one whose "path" is positively described as "paved." This person, however, is not said to be the "diligent" person as one might expect, but the morally "upright" person.

These sayings confirm that the sages of Proverbs regarded their instruction about laziness and diligence, not in terms of how we can get ahead economically and avoid fiscal shortfalls, but rather primarily in terms of their larger moral project of delineating what virtues belong to the way of wisdom. One further saying about laziness and diligence confirms this in a striking way and highlights the subtlety and artistry of the sages' teaching. Proverbs 12:27 reads:

> The lazy do not roast their game, but the diligent obtain precious wealth. (NRSV)

This translation of the proverb makes it sound much like the other lazy-diligent sayings that use wealth and poverty language, as we discussed above. But there are some textual problems in the verse that, when clarified, will help us see even more clearly how concerned the sages were with promoting the virtue of diligence, not in tracing the origins of rich and poor people. The Hebrew of the verse can be literally, even if awkwardly, translated as follows:

> A lazy person does not roast his game, but the wealth of a man precious diligent.

Although the term for "roast" is difficult, most scholars agree that this is the correct reading. With regard to the second line of the verse, however, there are a range of suggestions as to how the Hebrew might be rearranged or emended to make more sense. The NRSV, for instance, appears to import into the line the verb *obtain,* which is not in the Hebrew text. Why? Perhaps because many interpreters believe Proverbs promises a kind of literal wealth to those who become wise.

The great medieval Jewish scholar Rashi (1040–1105) suggested that the second half of the verse should not be emended as seen in the NRSV. Instead, Rashi contended that it should be translated as follows: "but the precious wealth of a person is [to be] diligent," with the adjective "precious" modifying the phrase "wealth of a person." If this understanding is correct, the sense of the verse is not that one who is diligent will gain money or wealth, as the NRSV translation implies. Rather the line describes what is truly or genuinely valuable for a person, namely "to be diligent"; that is, to be a person of virtue.

This way of understanding the line finds further support if we look to the overall literary context of Proverbs. You may recall that in Proverbs 1 (see pp. 27–30) the robbers claimed that their way, the wrong way of folly and wickedness, would produce "precious wealth." The Hebrew in Proverbs 12:27 uses the same words for both "precious" and "wealth" as the robbers do at the outset of the book. The verse also reminds us of Wisdom's own claim in 8:18 (see p. 48) that she holds real or "enduring" wealth—that which is of greatest value in life. Again the term Wisdom uses for *wealth* in 8:18 is the same as the word used in 12:27 and by the robbers in chapter 1. It's interesting to note, too, that in classical Hebrew one word for *gold* is spelled exactly like the word for *diligent* in 12:27. We might suspect then, that the sages, whom we know made good use of tropes and figures in their instruction, are engaging in a subtle form of wordplay. That is, a reader of Hebrew might initially think the proverb says that "The precious wealth of a person is gold," which is a kind of common sense, true statement when taken literally; it also essentially corresponds to the robbers' view. But through their artful play on words, the sages who have spoken so much about the value of diligence ask you to read again and thus understand that what is most valuable in life is not more and more gold, or precious wealth, but the virtues of wisdom's way, virtues like diligence.

For us today, understanding Proverbs' teaching about laziness and diligence in the context of the whole book means not only working diligently at whatever we do. It also means remembering that only with some violence to the moral system that the sages constructed can such proverbs be used to support a prosperity gospel perspective, which blames the poor for the moral deficiency that is believed to cause their poverty and lauds the rich for the virtue that their wealth supposedly affirms. Yet, more than this, if Proverbs' teaching on laziness and diligence does not offer simple explanations of how rich and poor people come about, we are reminded again that the sages did not brook simplistic answers to complicated questions, and neither should we. The sages' perspectives were rather bound up within a whole system of moral value that placed special importance on social virtue, and as we shall see in chapter 4, a special concern for the poor. This social concern was the moral norm or standard that the sages articulated for us and claimed was built into the cosmos. It is against such norms that we today ought to understand all their moral teaching, especially any teaching that touches on economic matters, as do the lazy-diligent proverbs. The sages' clear set of moral norms also asks us to evaluate the criteria we use when thinking about our money and our economy to ensure that these criteria are consonant with the wisdom the sages claim infuses all of creation.

CHAPTER 4

Social Justice in the Book of Proverbs

The sages of Proverbs knew that humans must have a degree of material security in order to flourish. If you are destitute and cannot access the fundamental necessities of life, such as food and shelter, any talk about how "money can't buy you happiness" is hollow. The way of wisdom, from generosity to right speech, has at its core a relational component, which we have broadly been calling *social virtue*. Not surprisingly, Proverbs uses its vocabulary of money to describe the enduring worth of this social component of wisdom's way. Yet throughout the Bible, *social virtue* or *justice* largely revolves around questions of economic justice and involves most fundamentally a concern for the poor and other vulnerable people in society—questions we are still grappling with today.

The sayings in Proverbs that highlight different facets of social justice teach us practical things about money and the way of wisdom, including how we ought to use our money and how we ought to act when it comes to the full range of our economic dealings. In this chapter, we will examine the sages' advice about these issues, from our attitudes toward the poor and other socially vulnerable groups, to the duty of political leaders to ensure economic justice, to the question of justice in the marketplace—borrowing and lending, and the giving of bribes and gifts.

Kindness to the Poor and Vulnerable

The Book of Proverbs vigorously promotes the social virtue of extending kindness to the poor. The sages have much to say about how those who are not poor ought to treat those with fewer economic resources.

> Whoever oppresses the poor insults his Maker, but
> whoever is kind to the needy honors him. (Proverbs 14:31;
> cf. NRSV)

> Those who mock the poor insult their Maker; those who
> are glad at calamity will not go unpunished.
> (Proverbs 17:5; NRSV)

In these proverbs the sages draw a direct parallel between our conduct toward the poor and our conduct toward God. Oppressing and mocking the poor is an offense to the Deity, while showing kindness to the destitute is a demonstration of respect and concern for the Divine. Some readers—especially Christians—may recall that the Jewish sage we quoted above, Jesus of Nazareth, articulated a similar perspective. In the great judgment scene of Matthew 25, the exalted king—likely the Divine—evaluates human actions toward the poor, outcast, and vulnerable in this way: "And the king will answer them, 'Truly I tell you, just as you did it to one of the least of these who are members of my family, you did it to me.'" (Matthew 25:40; NRSV)

In other proverbs, the sages connect our actions or lack of actions, on behalf of the poor, not simply to the Divine, but to certain consequences.

Whoever stops his ears at the cry of the wretched; he too will call and not be answered. (Proverbs 21:13)

Those who are generous are blessed, for they share their bread with the poor. (Proverbs 22:9; NRSV)

The one who gives to the poor will not be in want. But whoever shuts his eyes will have many curses. (Proverbs 28:27)

As with the other verses in Proverbs that seem to promise literal wealth to those whose lives are guided by wisdom, we are not dealing here with a question of whether the rewards and punishments sketched in the sayings regularly do or do not literally come about. Rather, these sayings seek to motivate us to get on the right moral side of the cosmos. Showing kindness to the poor and generously giving to the needy belong to the way of wisdom and so are rhetorically linked to the positive images of blessing and abundance in the verses. Ignoring or oppressing the poor belongs to the way of folly and wickedness and is thus associated with curses and a person's fruitless calls for aid.

What is at stake for the poor in all this are the basic necessities of physical existence, which in Proverbs 22:9 is represented as access to "bread," a fundamental staple and symbol of life. What is at stake for the audience, the ones who, like many of us today, are actually in a position to give generously to the needy, is the meaningful and full life to which the way of wisdom leads. In today's world about 12 percent of the population in the United States lives in poverty and up to 50 percent of the population of the globe subsists on less than $2 a day.[1] So there is ample opportunity to explore this stretch of the path of wisdom, which is characterized by the virtue of showing kindness to the poor. Of course, many of our local churches and synagogues, as well as a host of community organizations, from homeless shelters to job placement programs, work tirelessly on behalf of poor and struggling people. Partnering with and supporting the work of these groups—not to mention larger institutions, such as UNICEF (the United Nations Children's Fund), which works to ensure that impoverished children across the globe receive basic nutrition, health care, and a host of other services—makes kindness to the poor a relatively simple first step along the path of wisdom.

The Rights of the Poor

The cluster of sayings in Proverbs that we just examined highlight the sages' concern that the wise and righteous attend to the real material needs of the poor. Two further proverbs speak of another sort of obligation to the poor.

> Do not rob the poor person because he is a poor person;
> do not crush the lowly person in the gate. (Proverbs 22:22)

> The righteous know the rights of the poor; the wicked have
> no such understanding. (Proverbs 29:7; NRSV)

In these lines, the sages are offering specific instruction concerning our obligation to the poor in the *legal* realm. In Proverbs 22:22, for instance, the sages not only prohibit us from robbing a poor person, but they censure the "crushing" of the poor "in the gate," a pointed reference to that place in ancient Israel where legal disputes were heard and adjudicated. Similarly Proverbs 29:7 deploys legal terminology when it refers to the "rights" of the poor and the fact that the "righteous" person will acknowledge these rights.

It is easy to hear the sages' prophetic voice in these verses about the treatment of the poor. They recognized the economic vulnerability of the poor as well as their vulnerability in the legal system, and demanded that steps be taken to ensure that they would be protected. As the sages saw it, the follower of the way of wisdom seeks to ensure that no one might "rob the poor" (22:22) of their due, but that all "know" or acknowledge the "rights" of the needy (29:7).

In today's world we can discern any number of analogies to this aspect of the sages' teaching. The poor are disadvantaged in our legal system, not only because they lack the resources to mount a defense the way the wealthy do, or to contend for justice with well-fixed institutions and individuals. They are also disadvantaged more fundamentally because our laws and institutions are often set up, or at least appear to be set up, to serve the economically powerful first and foremost, leaving the needs of struggling working people and the destitute unanswered.

Most minimum wage laws, for example, have not kept pace with the cost of living. Many across a broad class spectrum contend that tax laws favor the wealthy with a variety of loopholes not available to those who make less than $50,000 annually. Immigration laws bar poor workers from poor countries from entering rich countries legally, forcing many to risk their lives to enter a foreign land to find work by which they might better support their families or simply seek a better life. Meanwhile businesses that employ undocumented workers benefit from (and sometimes exploit) the cheap labor they provide, skirting toothless enforcement of labor laws. Government intervention to bail out floundering investment firms, such as Bear Stearns in 2008, are swift, while thousands of working- and middle-class homeowners caught in the subprime mortgage crisis of 2007–2008 believe government help has been too little. Erudite thinkers such as Joseph Stiglitz, mentioned earlier, write book-length studies, arguing that international financial institutions, such as the International Monetary Fund and the World Trade Organization—enterprises ostensibly created to assist poor, developing nations—actually work on behalf of international investors. All this, along with the periodic outcries about well-financed lobbyists representing special interests and making political contributions to sway lawmakers, show us—if we are truly willing to see—how much economic power distorts matters in the legal realm to the advantage of the wealthy and powerful.

Of course, every example mentioned above is enormously complex. Economic experts and pundits alike will disagree about whether one policy or project benefits the wealthy, the middle class, or the poor. They will remind us that an increase in the minimum wage may hurt small businesses, which then won't be able to employ anyone. They will force us to think about whether and why the wealthy in our society actually should pay more taxes or not. They will ask us to think about what our obligation to other countries and foreign workers is or ought to be in a globalized world.

The economic world from which the Book of Proverbs comes to us was not nearly as complex as ours. We cannot reduce the complexity of our world, and the sages of Proverbs do not necessarily ask us to. They do, however, demand that we genuinely seek to heed and respond to the cries of the poor and their advocates. By doing so, we can discern how, both as individuals and as a society of great wealth, our economic ways depart from wisdom's ways—perhaps via institutional and economic arrangements that are so ingrained in our system and psyches as to be all but invisible to us. As Proverbs 13:23 notes, "The field of the poor may yield much food, but it is swept away through injustice" (NRSV). By listening to the poor and their advocates, we can begin to question our assumptions and discover what we might do to return to the righteous path.

The sages' norm, the standard by which they measured their individual and collective economic life, was the standard of *tzedek, mishpat,* and *meysharim*—social justice, righteousness, and equity

(Proverbs 1:3, p. 23). The question for us today is whether this is our standard as well. Do we ask ourselves, as well as our experts and policy makers, whether the way we use our money and the laws and rules we create to arrange our economy truly bend toward justice for the poor and needy of our world? Or are we content to stop our ears (Proverbs 21:13, p. 87), shut our eyes (Proverbs 28:27, p. 87), and turn a blind eye to the fate of the poor in the face of incontrovertible evidence of national and global poverty? Are we content to continue believing that current arrangements which so obviously benefit those of us who are most well off, will at some point—somehow—begin to work for the most needy as well?

In the eighth century BCE, the great Israelite prophet Isaiah recognized how the economic and political powers of his society exerted control—illegitimately, in his view—over legal and economic institutions for their own advantage. Isaiah well understood how this sort of corruption worked at the expense of the poor. And he denounced it.

> Ah, you who make iniquitous decrees, who write oppressive statues, to turn aside the needy from justice and to rob the poor of my people of their right.... (Isaiah 10:1–2; NRSV)[2]

Other Socially Vulnerable Groups

Like other books of the Bible, Proverbs recognizes that those who seek wisdom's way of justice will be concerned not only with the protection of the poor, but also with the well-being of other socially marginalized people. In the patriarchal world of ancient Israel (and other cultures), such marginalized groups typically included widows and orphans—those who had no male head of household responsible for ensuring their economic and social well-being.[3] The sages speak specifically of the wise and just person's responsibilities to these groups.

> The Lord tears down the house of the arrogant, but maintains the widow's boundaries. (Proverbs 15:25; cf. NRSV)

> Don't remove an ancient boundary marker, and don't invade the field of orphans, for their redeemer is strong; he will plead their cause against you. (Proverbs 23:10–11; cf. NRSV)[4]

In ancient Israel, widows and orphans were often easy targets for predators seeking economic advantage by encroaching on their holdings. Proverbs 15:25 and 23:10–11 both employ the language of "boundaries" or "boundary marker" to imagine situations where the property or land of a widow or orphan is illegitimately impinged upon by another. Proverbs 23:10 explicitly commands that such a thing should never be done and reminds readers that while orphans may lack a human figure to protect them, their well-being is nonetheless ensured by a higher power, and the one who will plead the case of the orphans is amply able to do so. According to the sages, "their redeemer is strong," words that are a clear allusion to the Divine. Proverbs 15:25, by contrast, claims that God is the one who establishes the boundary of a widow's land and uproots the "house of the arrogant." The parallelism of the two halves of the verse implies that this arrogant person is the very one attempting to gain personal advantage by seizing the land of the widow. The arrogance of his character is revealed by his willingness to attack a vulnerable person to enlarge his own holdings.

Thus, for the sages, it is none other than God who protects the interests of widows and orphans. For Proverbs, the wise and righteous person did the same. In our world, widows and orphans in many instances remain socially and economically vulnerable, like the poor. Those who follow wisdom's way today will, like the sages of old, be concerned with the well-being of such people.

However, beyond addressing the plight of widows and orphans, the sages also ask us to consider who else in our world, around the block, and around the globe, is socially or economically marginalized. According to the National Runaway Switchboard in the United States alone between 1.6 million and 2.8 million young people run away from their homes every year (for a range of reasons).[5] Thousands end up on the streets of our big cities, homeless and vulnerable to violent crime, drug addiction, and sexual exploitation. Meanwhile, the U.S. government reports that more than 800,000 people are "trafficked" across international borders annually while millions more are trafficked within their own countries—to serve as indentured laborers or, as the U.S. Conference of Catholic Bishops says, as slaves.[6] Like ancient Israel's widows and orphans, the victims of human trafficking are usually women and children. The sages would likely insist that we consider well how these others are protected or exploited and be clear about our responsibility to work on their behalf. Organizations like Covenant House, which in twenty-one cities across the United States and beyond offers food, shelter, and a range of other services to runaway youth, exemplify how to put the sages' mandates into action.[7] Humantrafficking.org, a webpage of the Academy for Educational Development, and a host of other organizations likewise advocate forcefully on behalf of those sold into modern-day slavery. To support the work of such groups would be a way to embark on wisdom's path.

The King's Duty

Besides insisting that we show kindness to the disadvantaged and other marginalized groups, and ensure that these socially and economically vulnerable people are treated fairly in the legal system, the sages of Proverbs also offer us counsel about the role of political authorities in establishing and maintaining justice in a community or society.

The sages knew well that unjust political leaders can devastate those over whom they wield authority, especially the vulnerable poor. Proverbs 28:16, for instance, claims:

A prince who lacks understanding is very oppressive; he who spurns ill-gotten gains will live long.

In this verse the sages make clear that the tyrannical "prince" is one who is *not* following the way of wisdom. This political leader "lacks" the "understanding" characteristic of the wise and righteous. By contrast, the ruler who forgoes and rejects "ill-gotten gains" (*betsa'*)—the same phrase that the teacher or father used in Proverbs 1 (see pp. 27–28) to describe the "sinner's" violent quest for wealth—will have a fruitful life and will "live long." His kingdom will be established.

Another verse in Proverbs describes the "wicked ruler," most likely a political figure, as a threatening wild beast.[8]

A roaring lion and a prowling bear is a wicked man ruling a poor person. (Proverbs 28:15)

A further proverb offers other violent images to describe political rulers who brutally wield power against their vulnerable subjects to serve their own selfish interests. They are:

A breed whose teeth are swords and whose jaws are knives ready to devour the poor of the land, the needy among humans. (Proverbs 30:14)

By contrast, Proverbs 31:8–9, which is an address by a queen mother to her royal son named Lemuel, speaks more positively of the roles and duties of the king. She exhorts her son:

> Speak up for the dumb, for the rights of all the unfortunate.
> Speak up, judge righteously, champion the poor and needy.

Likewise, Proverbs 29:14 notes:

> A king who judges the poor honestly, his throne will be established forever.

By including the words of Lemuel's mother in 31:8–9 and sayings like 29:14 in their book, the sages of Proverbs assert that the king, or the political elite of a society, has a special obligation to ensure the well-being of the poor, both economically and socially—including in the legal realm—as the language of "rights" and "judging" in the verses suggests. Political leaders are charged with actively ensuring that the rights of the poor are protected, and even promoting their cause, a view that is also common in other parts of the Bible and the ancient Near East generally.[9]

We might imagine that, in the twentieth century, the sages of Proverbs would have largely approved of the administration of Franklin Delano Roosevelt, whose 1930s-era New Deal policies focused on doing just that—both bolstering the American economy, which was mired in the Great Depression, and promoting the cause of ordinary Americans. His policies of banking reform, agricultural stimuli, labor union support, work relief programs, and Social Security helped lift the poor out of poverty and improve the overall health of the country's economy.

Interestingly in Proverbs 29:14 the sages note that political leaders who ensure justice for the poor exercise legitimate dominion. Such a ruler's "throne" will be "established forever." Yet what the sages imply, but leave unsaid, in this regard is just as important. The rule of the political leader who does not fulfill his

obligation to guarantee social justice in his realm, to provide for
the poor, and care for widows and orphans, will not last long.
This sort of ruler is, in essence, illegitimate; one could assume that
the sages would feel no moral obligation to remain uncritically
subservient to such an authority. Such a regime, the sages promise
us, will not last. The sages' rhetoric is a statement of their moral
position, not a prediction. Unjust leaders follow the way of folly
and wickedness and hence their reigns *ought not* to endure long.
The reign of just kings *ought* to endure because they act in accord
with wisdom.

Other verses in Proverbs that do not explicitly mention the poor
nonetheless indicate that a leader's rule is legitimate only insofar as
the leader establishes and maintains social justice.

> Wicked deeds are an abomination to kings, for by justice is
> a throne established. (Proverbs 16:12)

Proverbs 20:28 similarly alludes to the king's "covenant" obligation.
This, at least in part, may refer to the king's responsibility to maintain justice. It is upon this "steadfast love" that the monarch's rule
or "throne" rests:

> Steadfast love and truth preserve the king and his throne is
> upheld by steadfast love.

Proverbs 25:4–5, too, observes the key role of justice in grounding a
leader's rule:

> Take away the wicked from the presence of the king and his
> throne will be established in justice. (cf. NRSV)

And according to Proverbs 29:4:

> A king with justice causes the land to endure, but the tax man tears it down.[10]

The implication of this last verse is that the taxes in question are unjustly levied or that the tax collector collects more than is legitimate.

According to the sages, a king (and by extrapolation, any political leader) is responsible for providing justice to those who seek it. This justice is grounded in the divine order of things. Proverbs asserts that when political rulers promote and ensure genuine social justice, they align themselves with the divine will.

> Many are those who seek the face of the ruler, but justice for humanity is from the Lord. (Proverbs 29:26)[11]

In Proverbs 8:15, the wisdom by which the Divine created the cosmos says:

> By me kings reign, and rulers decree what is just;
> By me rulers rule, and nobles, all who govern rightly.
> (NRSV)

What are the contemporary implications of this call for justice? This is a very tricky question, since the political order the sages lived through and imagined was very different from the kind of society in which most readers of this book live. We find ourselves in a liberal democracy that values highly, and even mandates, the separation of religion and government (often called "church and state"). As the so-called establishment clause of the First Amendment of the U.S.

Constitution puts it, "Congress shall make no law respecting the establishment of religion...." Ancient Israel, however, was structured as a theocracy, with the king serving as God's viceroy or representative on earth. All of the sages' claims about the role and legitimacy of political rulers emerge from, and need to be evaluated in light of, this context.

For some people today that quintessential liberal, political value—the separation of religion and state—means that citizens of modern, liberal states must bracket all things religious, including religious values, if and when they want to participate in the political processes of their nation. However, some scholars believe that the principle of religion-state separation does not require citizens to check their religious perspectives at the entrance to the political arena. Rather, religious people of all faiths have the right to bring their religious values to public debates and then have those values tested and refined by interaction with the values of others—religious or secular. In this view, all voices can be heard and the voices of all ought to be protected and permitted a hearing.[12]

One way of thinking about the contemporary import of the sages' teaching regarding the duties of political leaders is to consider how the values of the sages intersect, or collide, with our own political values. Whether in today's world you are inclined to believe more "liberally" that government has a significant role to play in maintaining social welfare, or whether you take a more "conservative" view of such intervention as government meddling, the sages' words can challenge all of us. They can urge us to consider whether, or to what extent, some of our deeply held political values and beliefs about money and economics are in line with Proverbs' way of virtue. The sages can challenge those of us who desire to travel the path of wisdom, who seek the well-being and fullness of life that wisdom promises, to deploy our intellectual virtues in looking at ourselves and our own interests through the prism of the sages' words; we can abandon our ideologies concerning money, economics, wisdom, and justice and consider which outcomes of which policies more closely approximate Proverbs' vision of a social realm characterized by justice and equity (cf. Proverbs 1:3, p. 23), as did the Civil Rights Act of 1964 and the Voting Rights Act of 1965. The sages' words can and ought to prompt us to consider to what extent we may want to recalibrate our political and economic values to align more with wisdom's way.

Justice in the Marketplace

Besides the calls to show kindness to the poor and vulnerable people in our midst and the claim that a society's political leaders have a responsibility to maintain social justice in their realms, a number of other sayings in the Book of Proverbs offer us a different sort of practical advice about economic matters. These proverbs speak of every person's responsibility to act in a way that is fair, honest, and just when it comes to basic economic activity like buying and selling.

> False scales are an abomination to the Lord; an honest weight pleases him. (Proverbs 11:1)

> Just scales and balances are the Lord's; all the weights in the bag are his work. (Proverbs 16:11)

> False weights and false measures; both are an abomination to the Lord. (Proverbs 20:10)

> False weights are an abomination to the Lord; dishonest scales are not good. (Proverbs 20:23)

Each of these sayings about weights and balances reflects the context of the ancient marketplace, where the value for goods bought and sold was measured on a scale. These ancient scales consisted of a horizontal beam placed over a central fulcrum. Attached to the beam were pans or hooks upon which objects, including precious metals, were weighed or balanced. In Jeremiah 32:10, for instance, we find the prophet Jeremiah weighing out some silver that he was to use in the purchase of a plot of land.[13]

> I signed the deed, sealed it, got witnesses, and weighed the money on scales. (NRSV)

In the proverbs cited above, the sages explicitly and repeatedly insist that those who seek wisdom's benefits will not engage in deceptive economic practices; they will not use false scales and false weights. These practices are "not good," according to Proverbs 20:23. Proverbs 11:1 and 20:10, however, use even stronger language to describe how much the sages wanted to teach their students—and us today—to avoid any sort of cheating in economic dealings. These lines call such actions "an abomination to the Lord."

The sages' emphasis on honesty in marketplace activities can serve as a further moral principle by which we who wish to travel wisdom's way today might measure our economic activities as well. However, as I will suggest more specifically below, given the great difference between our context and the sages' world, we may need to be quite intentional about the specific ways we go about this.

Borrowing, Lending, and Surety

The sages of Proverbs also offer practical instruction regarding borrowing and lending, and especially about "standing surety" or guaranteeing that the loan of a third party will be repaid to the creditor. The verses that treat these matters consistently urge readers to avoid getting mixed up in this sort of business, highlighting its risky nature, though I will suggest a more fundamental moral principle underlying this practical reason. Proverbs 6:1–5, for instance, says:

> [1]My son, if you provide surety to your neighbor, if you
> clap hands for a stranger;
> [2]If you have ensnared yourself by the words of your mouth,
> if you are captured by the words of your mouth;
> [3]Do this, then, my son, and save yourself, for you have come
> into the hand of your neighbor. Go grovel and badger your
> neighbor.
> [4]Do not give sleep to your eyes nor slumber to your
> eyelids.
> [5]Escape like a gazelle from a hunter, like a bird from the
> hand of the fowler.[14]

On an initial reading of this passage, it is difficult to discern precisely what situation the teaching voice, or father, is imagining. Who is the lender? Who is the borrower? Who is standing surety? And what is this business of clapping hands, and birds escaping from fowlers?[15]

Although some scholars take a different view, the passage most likely envisions the "neighbor" to be the lender and the "stranger" to be the borrower, since in verse 3, the addressee falls into the hand (or power) of the neighbor. As a lender, the neighbor would be able to demand payment from the guarantor. The addressee is thus the guarantor—the one who, with his own money or property, will guarantee that the neighbor is repaid if the stranger defaults on his loan. The action of "clapping the hands" likely was a symbolic gesture to seal an agreement, perhaps analogous to the way some of us today agree to something when we "shake on it." We should also note that the stranger in these lines is not necessarily an ethnic or national

foreigner, a non-Israelite. Rather, this person is probably just someone the addressee doesn't know, someone from a different town or
village. In any case, the father or teacher urges the addressee, who
might have stood surety for a stranger's loan, to make a concerted
effort to be released from his obligation. He should forgo sleep to
petition and plead with his neighbor until he is released from the
responsibility. The images from the world of hunting and fowling at
the end of the passage indicate just how risky the father or teacher
thinks standing surety in this way—for a stranger—is: It endangers
the son's very life.

Other sayings in Proverbs likewise underscore the peculiar risk
of standing surety.

> To guarantee loans for a stranger brings trouble, but there
> is safety in refusing to do so. (Proverbs 11:15; NRSV)

> Take the garment of the one who has given surety for a
> stranger; seize the pledge given as surety for foreigners.
> (Proverbs 20:16; NRSV)[16]

> Do not be one of those who give their hand, who stand
> surety for debts, lest your bed be taken from under you
> when you have no money to pay. (Proverbs 22:26–27;
> cf. JPS).

The first of these verses notes that those who stand surety for a
stranger are in for trouble, but promises security to the one who
refrains from such practices. The second one simply commands that
the property or pledge of one who stands surety for an unknown person be confiscated, even though there is no mention that the borrower has, in fact, defaulted on the loan. The sages, it seems, are so

sure that this person would lose his property that they order it taken from him ahead of time. The last two verses, Proverbs 22:26–27, warns of the price a guarantor may have to pay if the debtor is unable to pay back the loan when the creditor seeks repayment. If the guarantor is not able to fulfill this financial obligation, his property—in this case his bed!—will be seized.

For the sages of Proverbs, to stand surety, especially for a stranger, is economically very risky. As some of us know from personal experience, strangers who borrow money are more likely to disappear than those with solid roots in the community. For Proverbs, those who avoid standing surety guard their way and exercise one of wisdom's *practical* virtues.

Yet if standing surety were so risky, why would anyone be tempted to engage in the practice in the first place? As it turns out, in the ancient world, as in ours, a person would stand surety for another for one of two reasons. One might do so out of compassion, to help out another, as the later Jewish sage, Jesus Ben Sira (or Sirach) noted (Sirach 29:14, p. 105). Alternatively, one might stand surety in order to make a profit by charging a fee for doing so.[17]

However, if the motivation for guaranteeing a loan was to profit from it, the sages' opposition to the practice may not have been merely practical. Their opposition may also reflect a concern to rein in the addressee's quest for wealth and thereby reorient her to a better understanding of money and its relationship to the way of wisdom. We have already seen that the sages discourage any arduous or overly zealous pursuit of wealth, and especially condemn any quest for money or riches that might involve injustice. Interestingly, Proverbs 28:8 suggests that the sages viewed the profit motive in borrowing and lending scenarios as something that was inherently unjust, even if the verse doesn't speak specifically of the practice of standing surety for profit. Those who seek gain through working the system of borrowing and lending, the sages claim, will not find it. Instead, in the sages' moral imagination, what they accumulate will, ironically, benefit the most needy.

> The one who increases his wealth by loans at discount or interest amasses it for one who is generous to the poor. (Proverbs 28:8; cf. JPS)

Proverbs 28:8 is obviously a paradoxical statement. It is a clear example of one of those tropes and figures the Prologue told us to expect to find in the book. We thus ought not to be too concerned about finding real-life examples of, or figuring out, how and when a generous person will benefit from those who seek to profit by lending at interest. Rather we should consider how the moral thrust of the verse fits into the broader moral system the sages develop throughout Proverbs.

The sages here suggest that the effort to gain an economic advantage from others' need—in this case the need for a loan—does not profit; it has no value and thus belongs to the way of folly. By contrast, generosity to the poor does profit, it does have value and, hence, belongs to wisdom's path. By identifying the moral principles at work in the sages' teaching, we can use them as a standard by which we evaluate the way we use our money today. I now turn to a test case, also from antiquity, that serves as a model for how we might adapt the principle to our own time and place.

Developing Wisdom

It is interesting to note that the Jewish scribe mentioned above, Jesus Ben Sira (or Sirach), takes a slightly different view on guaranteeing loans in his book than Proverbs does. He builds on Proverbs' teaching and updates it for his own day, thereby providing a model for us when thinking about how we might best adopt and translate wisdom's way for our day.

Sirach lived and worked in Jerusalem around 175 BCE, when Jews were ruled by the Greek Seleucid kingdom. During this time of increased trade and economic activity, when many people were economically vulnerable, Sirach was less concerned that his students might seek to make a profit by standing surety for strangers and more concerned about offering advice about the practice undertaken for the benefit of a neighbor. For Sirach, it was entirely appropriate, even if risky, to stand surety on behalf of one's neighbor who was in need.

> A good person will be surety for his neighbor,
> But the one who has lost all sense of shame will fail him.
> (Sirach 29:14; NRSV)

> Assist your neighbor to the best of your ability,
> But be careful not to fall yourself (Sirach 29:20; NRSV)

This was especially true if that neighbor was reliable and took seriously the risks the guarantor was incurring on his behalf. Hence, Sirach instructed his students not only to be good givers but to be moral *receivers* as well.

> Do not forget the kindness of your guarantor,
> for he has given his life for you.
> A sinner wastes the property of his guarantor.
> (Sirach 9:15–16; NRSV)

Moreover, Sirach is also explicit that a guarantor ought not to seek to profit from standing surety for another. He calls the one who strives after such profit a "sinner," just like the one who "wastes the property of his guarantor."

> The sinner comes to grief through surety;
> his pursuit of gain involves him in lawsuits.
> (Sirach 29:19; NRSV)

Sirach thus agrees with the earlier sages of Proverbs that standing surety can be risky and that some might wrongly pursue it for profit. For Sirach, however, living and thinking in a different context than the sages of Proverbs, if standing surety is something that will help out a neighbor in need and that neighbor is responsible, the risks are acceptable. The social benefit that accrues when one person helps another in need outweighs the financial risks to the guarantor. In this regard we can see how Sirach, like the sages of Proverbs, also places a premium on social virtue. Indeed, elsewhere Sirach, in a manner reminiscent of Proverbs, encourages his students to give alms to the poor and seek their well-being (cf., for example, Sirach 4:1–10).

Sirach's "extension" of the sage's wisdom is a valuable example for us. It offers a model of how we, too, might trace the trajectories of the sages' teaching for our day. Sirach didn't reject Proverbs' teaching about surety outright. Rather, he considered the principle behind the sages' censure of the practice—its risky nature, the fact that some do it only for profit—and brought that into critical dialogue with the sages' fundamental desire to promote social and economic solidarity as well as the situation of his own day.

One example of how some today are taking risks in borrowing and lending practices in order to promote the well-being of needy neighbors and hence the health of their broader communities is the microcredit movement. These programs, which often assist women, provide small loans (sometimes less than $100) to poor people, usually in developing countries. Because of their lack of credit history and collateral, these people would never qualify for loans from banks. Yet even this small amount of capital, when invested, for example, in animals like chickens and cows that will produce eggs and milk that a poor family can both consume and sell to generate income, can make a significant difference in the lives of many. While they may remain in poverty, their vulnerability may decline and their sense of self-esteem may rise. Today, via the Internet, virtually anyone can make a loan in a microcredit program through the work of organizations like Kiva (www.kiva.org). Such organizations allow you to make direct loans to individuals (often poor women) around the globe who need capital for small business projects that can significantly improve their own, and their family's, quality of life. Interestingly, some successful microcredit organizations, such as Mexico's *Compartamos* (Let's Share), have been shifting to "for profit" activity, forcing the microcredit world itself to wrestle with questions of economic motives in a way that is reminiscent of the issues the ancient sages struggled with.[18]

Bribes and Gifts

The ancient sages of Proverbs also taught their students, and by extension us today, about the efficacy of bribes and gifts. These scribes, who emphasized the worth of practical virtues (cf. Proverbs 1:4, p. 23) understood how their world worked and understood the value of gifts—how such presents could often open doors and smooth over difficult situations.

A bribe is like a magic stone in the eyes of those who give it; wherever they turn they prosper. (Proverbs 17:8; NRSV)

A gift opens doors; it gives access to the great.
(Proverbs 18:16; NRSV)

A gift in secret averts anger; and a concealed bribe in the
bosom, strong wrath. (Proverbs 21:14; NRSV)

However, despite their very practical and realistic understanding of
how bribes and gifts might ease our way in life, the sages did not necessarily recommend that their students pursue such a course of
action. Their overall evaluation of bribes and gifts was not based on
their obvious efficacy. Rather, the sages attempt to reckon how such
gift giving might or might not align with other virtues and values
belonging to wisdom's way, including social justice and equity. For
instance, the sages knew that gifts and bribes do not form a solid
foundation for enduring social relations (a theme we will return to
in chapter 5), but could merely be a strategy for self-promotion,
which would attract to the giver only hangers-on who are looking to
benefit themselves.

Many seek the favor of the generous and everyone is a
friend to a giver of gifts. (Proverbs 19:6; NRSV)

The sages also recognized that the temptation to enhance one's status might lead some to offer others economic advantage without,
apparently, being able to deliver on such promises.

Like clouds and wind without rain is one who boasts of a
gift never given. (Proverbs 25:14; NRSV)

The sages understood that the giving of gifts and bribes would fail to
provide a secure foundation for social relations: it could also

threaten the establishment of justice in a community. Hence, with a prophetic accent, they again spoke out against bribes.

> Those who are greedy for unjust gain make trouble for
> their households, but those who hate bribes will live.
> (Proverbs 15:27; NRSV)

> The wicked accept a concealed bribe to pervert the ways of
> justice. (Proverbs 17:23; NRSV)

With such proverbs the sages are clearly indicating that whenever the giving of a gift threatened social well-being or harmony, or gave a person an unfair advantage over others in matters of justice, this action belonged to the way of folly and wickedness. However, the sages of Proverbs also knew that the temptation to seek one's own advantage through gifts and bribes was, like the sinners' promise of "precious wealth" in Proverbs 1 (see pp. 27–30), a continual temptation for their audience. And they didn't shrink from boldly stating that fact.

> To show partiality is not good—yet for a piece of bread a
> person may do wrong. (Proverbs 28:21; NRSV)

Proverbs' Justice: Then and Now

In today's electronic age, many of us have less opportunity to cheat in the weighing out of the goods we buy, say, in the local supermarket, than the people of ancient Israel or the millions for whom traditional marketplaces remain the norm. Likewise many of us may not directly stand surety for others in order to make a profit, even if we may cosign loans for friends and family. Yet the sages of Proverbs, we can imagine, would still be concerned that the *principles* of fair and honest exchange that they advocate govern all our economic activity wherever, whenever, and however that might happen. Embodying these principles in today's world, however, may present considerable difficulties, given the immense complexity and scale of the economy that most of us participate in, either directly or indirectly and often anonymously.

The very size and complexity of the modern marketplace minimizes a sense of our own individual economic responsibility. It thus intensifies the need to reflect on whether the kinds of moral principles the sages associated with the way of wisdom, are celebrated or disregarded in our economic activities.

For instance, those of us who seek to follow the way of wisdom would do well to ask if the rules and practices of the financial markets where our portfolios and retirement savings are invested adequately reflect the principles the sages promote. The contemporary concern that the market provide investors with the highest short-term returns often compel businesses into practices that drive down wages so that some working people are forced to struggle to make a living wage. Barbara Ehrenreich's book *Nickel and Dimed: On (Not) Getting By in America* gives a powerful and poignant account of her (and others') effort to survive in the United States on low-wage work—from waitressing to working at Wal-Mart, the world's largest and most profitable retailer. Wal-Mart regularly comes under fire for its low wages, unaffordable health benefits, and aggressive efforts to keep workers from organizing. (Indeed, a government report charged the retailer with representing the "lowest common denominator in the treatment of working people.")[19] Likewise, the drive for high returns may promote the production of harmful but profitable products (guns, tobacco, alcohol) that have an especially negative impact on vulnerable poor people in our communities. This same bottom-line thinking may encourage questionable accounting practices that assure huge bonuses to corporate executives and potentially cost others greatly, as in the celebrated case of Enron. Such scandals in recent years have been nearly epidemic, running the gamut of well-known companies, from AOL Time Warner to Xerox.[20]

The arenas in which the modern market system operates also extend to areas that many of us would normally never think about, such as the buying and selling of home mortgages, as the subprime mortgage crisis of 2007–2008, noted above, has brought into sharp relief. Such conditions force us to ask ourselves to what extent our markets, and our participation in those markets, meet the minimum requirements of social justice imagined by the sages. This is so even if we are playing by the rules and according to the laws set up to govern those markets. For, like Isaiah, the sages knew that those who make the rules could make unjust rules.

All this forces us to ask ourselves how much we are willing to sacrifice economically to walk more fully and securely in wisdom's way of justice. Some of us might be willing to withdraw from contemporary economic arrangements and markets, opting out of the stock market and much of modern life. Some might even believe earnestly that revolution is necessary to build new a society and economic system that is more fundamentally in line with wisdom's way. However, for most of us such radical routes, because the different kinds of costs they would require, are not our first choice for realigning our personal and communal economic lives.

Yet the sages of old would likely ask us, "What *are* you willing to do?" Are we willing to pressure our elected officials to make new rules, or to pressure those who manage our money to shift our investing priorities? Are we willing to begin investing through socially conscious funds and supporting socially conscious businesses to leverage the strength of the market in order to reform market practices so that they more closely reflect the values of justice the ancient sages envisioned? Are we willing to investigate and then strive to change some of our purchasing habits, so that we can pressure manufacturers—who produce goods with sweatshop labor where workers struggle just to survive—to improve working conditions and wages?

Such strategies of consumer activism have resulted in some celebrated success stories. The grape boycott of the 1960s, which was instigated by César Chávez and the United Farm Workers to force grape growers to provide farm workers with fair work contracts, is perhaps the most dramatic of these cases. Millions of Americans who refused to buy grapes put great political and economic pressure on grape growers and aided the farm workers' cause. Such efforts continue, as is seen with the movement in some North American universities to pressure manufacturers of clothing with university logos to reform sweatshop labor practices. For example, one student group at the University of Michigan (SOLE; Students Organizing for Labor and Economic Equality) understands well how the global economic system functions and recognizes that in some parts of the world, workers' alternatives to sweatshop labor may be even less desirable. These students do not want to see the manufacturing jobs, which are often filled by desperately poor people, lost. Rather they seek to deploy the influence of their institutions to pressure manufacturers to improve wages and working conditions for their workers. The point is not to drive manufacturers elsewhere or to exploit other low-wage workers (a self-defeating scenario), but to use consumer influence to hold them accountable wherever their factories might be located.[21]

The sages of old would likely ask us if we are willing, through these methods and more, to take the sorts of actions that might make less economic sense for us, but align ourselves more closely with wisdom's vision of justice and money. As the spiritual mind of the twentieth century's greatest scientist, Albert Einstein, formulated it, "The most precious things in life are not those one gets with money" and "Only a life lived for others is a life worthwhile."[22]

CHAPTER 5

Discerning Wisdom and the Woman of Worth

We have seen how the sages of Proverbs help us recognize that wisdom's virtuous way is more valuable than any amount of money or any material goods that we might possess or seek. We have seen, too, that the ancient, wise scribes also insist that we fulfill our duties and obligations to the poor and vulnerable in society and that we act fairly and justly in all our economic dealings, whether we insist that the companies we invest in meet minimum requirements of justice or we join the efforts of advocates working to transform the lives of runaways or other vulnerable people. To the extent that any of us recognize this and subsequently act on wisdom's virtues, we begin to travel wisdom's path, a path the sages consistently imply will lead to good and positive results—not necessarily money and riches, but to an even more valuable, flourishing life, to what Woman Wisdom in Proverbs 8:18 (see p. 48) calls "enduring wealth."

The final set of sayings in the Book of Proverbs offer pointed observations about the real advantages wealth affords the rich and the real disadvantages the poor suffer in their poverty. These sayings round out our insights into the nature of the way of wisdom and how we might choose to walk its path.

The Sages' Critical Observations

Scholars of the Book of Proverbs often note that the ancient sages based much of their instruction, including their teaching about money and riches, on their observation of the social and natural world. Using observations about how things really are, they were able to articulate the best way of living. A famous passage that is often invoked as evidence for this view is Proverbs 24:30–34.

> [30]I passed by the field of one who was lazy,
>   by the vineyard of a stupid person;
> [31]and see, it was all overgrown with thorns;
>   the ground was covered with nettles,
>   and its stone wall was broken down.
> [32]Then I saw and considered it;
>   I looked and received instruction.
> [33]A little sleep, a little slumber,
>   a little folding of the hands to rest,
> [34]and poverty will come upon you like a robber,
>   and want, like an armed warrior.

In these lines a sage draws a conclusion from a situation that he presumably saw and offers a lesson about the value of diligence. Whether or not the teacher actually witnessed such a situation and then drew his conclusion, however, is not as important as the lesson he wants to instill in his students. (Recall that the sages often censure laziness and promote diligence through images of wealth and poverty.) The whole episode may be a rhetorical invention deployed to support the sage's point about the value of the virtue of diligence. Elsewhere in Proverbs, when the sages offer sayings that are cast essentially as observations, they regularly also carry an obvious rhetorical intent to instruct, functioning primarily as commands or exhortations to the hearer or reader to avoid one kind of activity and to pursue another.[1]

The sages' apparently unbiased observations are never truly neutral, however. Because they exist in a specific literary context, they are influenced by this context, which lends them meaning or gives them a particular moral slant.

Wealth's Advantages in Terms of Security

At least one saying in Proverbs appears to point out, plain and simple, the real advantage that wealth provides the rich in comparison to the obvious hardships that poverty brings on the poor.

> The wealth of the rich is their fortress; the ruin of the poor
> is their poverty. (Proverbs 10:15)

This verse observes that money or riches provide protection, or a safety net, to those who possess them. A rich person's wealth, for example, is called a "fortress," an image of protection and security. By contrast, the poverty of the poor person is called his "ruin"—a term that in another passage in the Bible, Jeremiah 48:39, describes the kind of suffering and utter destruction that comes to a people who are victims of a military rout. Money or riches can provide protection from personal catastrophes, or so the saying seems to suggest. Our own personal experiences may confirm such observations—for example, when we had enough reserve in our savings accounts to pay for unexpected major car or home repairs or a sudden illness, or worse. But there is more here than meets the eye.

Proverbs 13:8 expresses a similar perspective as 10:15, but with an interesting twist.

> Wealth is a ransom for a person's life, but the poor get no threats. (Proverbs 13:8; NRSV)

This verse also suggests that money provides a distinct advantage to those who possess it. The sages observe that riches can even save one's life, perhaps if a person is kidnapped and a ransom is demanded. On an initial reading then, it appears to contradict sayings like Proverbs 11:4 and 11:28 (both on p. 62) that we studied above, which claimed that wealth cannot "save." Yet recall early on in our study that we noted that proverbs that initially appear to contradict one another, can, on closer inspection sometimes form complementary components of a larger moral system.

Proverbs 13:8 notes not only that wealth is a ransom, but that "the poor get no threats." This statement, juxtaposed as it is with the first half of the verse, is not a mere observation. It offers a kind of implicit and critical *judgment* on the supposed advantages that wealth can provide. The sages affirm that, yes, a person with significant money might on occasion be able to buy back her or his life when it is threatened. Yet by observing that "the poor get no threats," Proverbs hints that it is precisely the possession of wealth that puts a person in such a precarious position in the first place. Ironically, wealth, which was thought to *protect* a rich person, turns out to *endanger* him. The poor person, whose poverty is normally viewed as demeaning, actually enjoys a kind of protection. She need not worry about being the target of extortion the way a person with significant wealth might, though the poor person remains vulnerable in other ways (e.g., in the legal realm, cf. chapter 4).

When we understand Proverbs 13:8 in this way we can also see, upon closer examination, that just as the second half of the verse qualified the first half of that line, so the first half of Proverbs 10:15, which speaks of the social protection wealth brings, is qualified by the second half of that verse. It observes that the "ruin" of the poor is their "poverty." But this, too, is not neutral language. The dire straits of the poor, as Proverbs 10:15 imagines them, reveal that there has been a failure in society, for the poor—as the sages have repeatedly argued—ought to be protected. In 10:15, however, there is no mention of their protection, only their vulnerability. When we consider the broader context of the book, we see that 10:15 is more than a mere observation—it is an *indictment* of those with wealth who have failed to fulfill their obligation to protect the vulnerable.

Other proverbs of "observation" operate in the same way, and are worth a second look. But what is the import of this? Some scholars conclude that Proverbs' teaching with regard to wealth and poverty is simply ambiguous, sometimes leaning in one direction and sometimes in another, much as a modern-day anthology of a particular culture's proverbs may preserve sayings that have a genuinely different point of view from one another.[2] Or it may be, as other commentators have suggested, that the sages included different sorts of sayings because these might reflect the different truths of the different situations that a student might encounter. The student who learns all the proverbs can draw on different sayings at the right moment. However, when the proverbs are understood in their primary (literary) context within the Book of Proverbs, another explanation is more likely. Although the sages recognize that oftentimes wealth does provide an advantage in the real world and that this is the way things *are,* the sages also assert that from the moral perspective of the path of wisdom, it is not the way things *ought to be.*

The sages challenge us to look more carefully and critically at the status quo in which we live, and to question whether the way our world operates is the way it ought to be operating. For example, the United States wields enormous economic, social, and military influence across the globe, often unilaterally. This provides us, as its citizens, with a sense of security, even power. On some level, we may begin to believe not just that this is the way things are, but that this is the way things should be. This, in turn, may encourage us to try to maintain our current advantages perhaps by endorsing (or by not questioning) current government policies. But how often do we consider that there might be other ways of ensuring our security in less invasive ways, ways that promote the building of a more global community? For instance, couldn't we step up our efforts to combat the global AIDS crisis or to forgive the debts of developing nations as the "Jubilee" (cf. Leviticus 25) movement promotes?[3] The path may not be easy, but it is impossible if we don't first critically examine the way things are.

We confirm Proverbs' parallel tracks—observing how the world is while simultaneously claiming that this is not the way the world should be—when we read Proverbs 10:15 (p. 117) together with Proverbs 18:10–11. Both speak of riches as a "fortress."

> [10]The name of the Lord is a tower of strength to which the
>   righteous person runs and is safe.
> [11]The wealth of the rich person is his fortress; in
>   his imagination, it is a protective wall.

In the second of these lines the sages of Proverbs get right to their point. Although wealth in the real world often appears to be a social buffer, an advantage in times of trouble, for the sages this is merely an illusion. Only in the rich person's "imagination" or "fancy" (as some translations put it) is money an advantage. The sages claim that despite the often real advantage wealth confers, it is nonetheless not the source of genuine security or well-being in life. Only the virtuous way of wisdom can give us true security, a point that is clear from the previous line (18:10). Whereas the "rich" person in this line seeks what the sages believe is a false refuge in the fortress of his money and riches, the "righteous" or "just" person seeks advantage and protection in the Lord. The just person, who trusts in God, is thus contrasted with the rich person who trusts in money. By explicitly naming the "rich" person, the sages are caricaturing the rich as the type of people who typically seek well-being in money, or who characteristically "trust" in wealth. To the modern imagination, such stereotypical images may include the soulless Wall Street power broker trading on insider information to buy and sell for his own benefit, regardless of the consequences to regular investors. For many, Michael Milken, dubbed the "junk bond king" of the 1980s, is the epitome of just such a figure.[4] The sages' clear implication is that the virtue of trust in God is superior to, more valuable than, the possession of riches. Recall that the Prologue told us at the very outset of the Book of Proverbs that "fear of the Lord" or a genuine piety or spirituality was a virtue that belonged preeminently to the way of wisdom. In short, genuine security comes not from money, but from following wisdom's way.

Another pair of verses takes this one step further.

The poor person speaks beseechingly. The rich person's answer is harsh. (Proverbs 18:23)

The rich person rules over the poor and the borrower is slave to the lender. (Proverbs 22:7)

Many of us might be able to remember, or imagine, situations when such proverbs were, or would be, literally true. Consider, for example, the petitions of immigrants who wish to enter foreign countries to work, but are met with the harsh reply that they should remain at home, languishing in poverty. And the subprime mortgage crisis, alluded to earlier, underscores precisely how borrowers are beholden to powerful lenders. However, again, when we read these types of observations in the broader literary context of Proverbs, the sayings begin to take on a more powerful rhetorical and moral force. For instance, when we recall that for the sages a primary obligation or virtue was to show kindness to the poor, not to lord it over or deal harshly with them, sayings like Proverbs 18:23 and 22:7 change from mere observations of social realities to strident critiques of those realities. Again, although the sayings may observe the way the world often is, they also implicitly teach us that the wise person knows that this is not the way the world should be. Like Proverbs 18:11, these sayings also mention explicitly the "rich" person and so once more may be negatively characterizing the "rich" as a type or class of people who typically treat the poor contemptuously. The "rich" person cited in Proverbs, we see again, is not the wise or virtuous person.

Wealth's Advantages in Social Settings

Besides offering financial and other types of security, wealth, according to still other sayings in Proverbs, offers *social* advantages as well. A number of proverbs, for instance, underscore the number (and nature) of the social ties that wealth can produce and that a lack of wealth can sever. Yet considering the context of the sages' broader teachings about wealth and poverty, we can see that rather than simply observing a social reality, these sayings likewise offer a powerful social critique.

> A poor person is despised even by his peers; but a rich person has many friends. (Proverbs 14:20)

Wealth makes many friends, but a poor person loses his last friend. (Proverbs 19:4)

Many court the favor of a great man, and all are the friends of a dispenser of gifts. (Proverbs 19:6)

All the brothers of a poor person despise him. How much more is he shunned by his friends.... (Proverbs 19:7)[5]

In the first three of these proverbs the rich person, or one with some form of riches ("wealth," "gifts") is associated with having multiple friends. Interestingly, if these aspects of the verses were read by themselves or in isolation from the rest of the book, we might think that the sages understood wealth's social effects to be exclusively positive. Yet the sayings are also explicit about the social effects of excessive lack; and these effects are exclusively negative. Poverty or being poor destroys fundamental social ties. It breaks up friendships (14:20; 19:4, 7) and can even destroy the bond of kinship (19:7). Some of us may know from experience the truth of these sorts of sayings when, perhaps, the many friends we enjoyed when we had money to burn suddenly evaporated when we found ourselves down on our luck. In some very real ways, the sages' observations about the friends of rich and poor people do reflect the way the world is.

However, the sages' teaching elsewhere in the book, about showing kindness to the poor, once again compels us to be suspicious of any understanding of the verses that emphasizes their nature as straightforward observations and their message as nothing more than a jaded, if realistic, observation of social realities. Proverbs 14:21 explicitly criticizes the situation described in verse 14:20, driving home the sages' point.

The one who despises his friend is wrong; the one who shows pity for the poor is happy. (Proverbs 14:21)

Verse 14:20 states an observation of how the world works—poor folks are despised, rich folks find friends—but verse 14:21 states more clearly the sages' fundamental perspective. It reveals how the "observation" of verse 14:20 is a subtle moral appraisal. The wise person will hold fast to the moral vision of verse 14:21 and reject the way of the world observed in verse 14:20 as not belonging to wisdom's path.

The sages' proverbs about the rich and their many friends also implicitly critique our social arrangements. If poverty sometimes diminishes the number of our social ties and if wealth increases our social ties, then the nature of the social ties that the rich person enjoys must be called into question. In the proverbs considered above, the social bonds or friendships that the rich person enjoys are likely rather weak. To understand fully the rhetorical force of the above proverbs, we must realize that the tie that binds the "friends" to the rich person are not the obligations and values of community or family, or the rich person's character. The only thing that supports those friendships is the rich person's possession of ephemeral wealth, the value of which the sages have persistently subordinated to virtue, especially social virtue.

Importantly, however, Proverbs not only observes how wealth might produce weak social ties and how poverty can endanger the bonds of kinship and friendship. The sages elsewhere also note what constitutes a positive or desirable scenario when it comes to one person's obligation to others, whether that person is a friend or a relative.

A friend loves at all times; a brother is born for adversity. (Proverbs 17:17)

> Do not abandon your own friend or the friend of your
> father....[6] (Proverbs 27:10)

Clearly, for the sages, the core value at the heart of their wisdom was healthy and committed social relationships.

Wealth and Fundamental Equality

Besides observing that the "rich" sometimes harshly relate to the poor and that wealth produces weak social ties, the sages of Proverbs also commented on other kinds of scenarios involving the rich and poor.

> A rich person and a poor person meet; the Lord is Maker
> of them all. (Proverbs 22:2; cf. NRSV)

> A poor person and a fraudulent person meet; the Lord gives
> light to the eyes of both of them. (Proverbs 29:13)

Only the first half of each of these verses might be said to resemble a genuine observation. The second half of each line, which speaks of the Divine's role in creating and sustaining humans, is more fundamentally a statement of faith.

Some scholars believe that the above sorts of sayings about God creating and giving life ("light to the eyes") to rich and poor alike indicate that the sages were attempting to justify social and economic differences, a perspective that may linger in our own attitudes.[7] If both rich and poor are created by God, after all, what can or should *we* do about it? Why should I undertake to work against, say, inner-city poverty if this is the way things are, if (in the words of a later Jewish sage, Jesus of Nazareth) "the poor you shall always have with you"? What would be the point?

However, when striving to understand these sorts of sayings, we should first of all remember Proverbs' other teaching about the "rich." As we have been discovering, Proverbs regularly associates these people with trusting too much in their wealth, lording it over the poor, and dealing harshly with the needy. (An exemplar of this kind of rich person is the greedy landlord and bank owner, Mr. Potter, in the classic 1946 film *It's a Wonderful Life*.) The parallel construction of Proverbs 22:2 and 29:13 carries forward the sages' critique of the "rich" as a type or class of person. In the first of these proverbs the poor person is simply and straightforwardly contrasted with the rich person. In the second proverb, however, the poor person meets a more overtly negative figure, a fraudulent person. Through this interchange between the rich person in the structure of the one verse and the fraudulent person in the structure of the other, the sages hint that the "rich" person is often "fraudulent."

Verses like 22:2 and 29:13 do not proclaim God's ordination of distinct classes or a divine division of humanity into haves and have-nots. As was the case with the lazy-diligent sayings, considered in chapter 3, these sayings are not attempts to understand why there are rich people and poor people. Although they may hint that some are poor because of the malice of others—as when the fraudulent person meets the poor person—these proverbs basically highlight the sages' belief in the fundamental equality of humans and the justice that is due them based on their common relationship to the Divine. All people, both rich and poor, owe their existence to the Creator, and this is something that precedes and transcends the distinctions that possession of greater or lesser degrees of wealth creates. This fundamental equality between humans, which the sages assert, also serves as the foundation for the sages' demand that the poor and other marginalized groups receive justice. For the sages of Proverbs, one's status as a creature of God determines one's worth or value, not one's economic or social circumstance.

Although this perspective may seem self-evident to those of us living in liberal democracies today, it was a radical idea when the sages conceived it, and it can still challenge us afresh. It can, for instance, remind us that our view of what it means that "all men are created equal" has required some revision over the centuries. In the United States the phrase excluded, in its original formulation, not only slaves from Africa and of African descent (not to mention the indigenous population of North America), but the female half of "humanity" as well. These people have not always been considered full members of U.S. society. Similar attitudes are still with us in the twenty-first century—perhaps expressed in more subtle, but nonetheless real ways—toward other groups of people who are generally regarded as outcasts from mainstream society. Such attitudes may be personal, cultural, or even government-sanctioned. This was allegedly the case in Atlanta when, prior to the 1996 Summer Olympics, the city was accused of systematically rounding up homeless men and women from the streets to remove them from public view and otherwise passing city ordinances that unfairly targeted the homeless and economically vulnerable.[8]

An Ironic Observation

Besides passing down proverbial observations that immediately ring true to most of us, the ancient sages of Proverbs also recorded sayings that at first glance many of us may not quickly comprehend. These sayings provide another and final invitation to us to engage the full range of the sages' wisdom. Proverbs 13:7 is one of these verses, which also speaks about rich and poor people. It especially needs to be considered both in light of the Prologue's claim that effort will be required to interpret the Book of Proverbs and in light of the way the sages elsewhere speak about wealth and poverty.

> One person shows himself to be rich and has nothing;
> another shows himself to be poor and has much wealth.
> (Proverbs 13:7; cf. JPS)

This statement of course might simply be a remark about how sometimes it is difficult to know for sure who is rich and who is poor. On the one hand, we may have heard tales of a rich person who lives a modest lifestyle, such as Wal-Mart founder Sam Walton, who—despite being a billionaire many times over—continued to drive a pickup truck and wore unassuming clothes from his own store.[9] On the other hand, we all know people who "put on airs" so they appear better off financially than they really are.

But it should be no surprise by now that behind the surface meaning of a proverb like 13:7, which tells us things aren't always what they seem, we might discern a more figurative understanding of the saying, one that underscores the sages' fundamental moral convictions. The rich person, though apparently in possession of much of what many of us believe is the key to security and well-being—money, or real material wealth—in reality doesn't hold anything of real value, *if* he is the type of rich person who acts fraudulently and harshly toward the poor. He only "shows himself to be rich." He only appears to enjoy security and the fullness of life. If the person of wealth is not on wisdom's path, he is by the sages' measure, and despite his money, fundamentally a poor wretch, a Scrooge. Likewise the poor person, who obviously lacks money or material goods, may nonetheless possess much of the sages' figurative "wealth," *if* he possesses wisdom's virtues, such as humility and a desire to live in peace and harmony with others. This person, though blessed with few economic resources, only "shows himself to be poor" since he is rich in virtue. For the sages, however, this figurative evaluation of the poor but richly wise person ought not to be taken as license for those who are wealthy to avoid responding responsibly to those who are materially poor.

Several final sayings that we have not yet considered in our study of money and the way of wisdom offer further observations or statements about wealth and poverty. Upon an initial reading, some people who possess a fundamental faith that the good will be recompensed with good will quickly see the truth of these sayings. However, many others of us will not immediately or easily recognize these proverbs as true to our experiences of real life.

> A good person causes his grandchildren to inherit; the
> wealth of sinners is stored up for the righteous.
> (Proverbs 13:22; cf. JPS)

> Oppressing the poor in order to enrich oneself, and giving
> to the rich will lead only to loss. (Proverbs 22:16; cf. NRSV)

It would, of course, be impossible to prove any of these observations by anything like a scientific study. It is not that the good person, as 13:22 calls him, the person on the way of wisdom, is one that is always prosperous enough to pass on his wealth to following generations— recall the poor but virtuous person just mentioned. And it is certainly not easy to verify that the wealth of sinners regularly goes to the righteous, and less so that unjust activity never profits the perpetrator, as Proverbs 22:16 suggests. In fact, it would probably be easier to prove the opposite of what these proverbs claim—that the wicked often do prosper.

It is difficult, if not impossible, to demonstrate the truth of these sorts of sayings because they are not genuine observations. These proverbs represent the fundamental perspective, or core beliefs, of the sages when it comes to much of their thinking about the virtuous way of wisdom. Like Dr. King's cosmic arc that bends toward justice, the sages' words reflect a fundamental faith that the genuine structure of the universe, which was created by wisdom, favors the life of virtue. This basic belief helps motivate those who choose wisdom's path to remain on it, by claiming that this way of life corresponds with reality. It is also an invitation, even to those of us who live in rich lands and possess much wealth, to embrace this same vision of reality, to forgo the ways of the "rich" and align our lives and actions with wisdom's way.

Full Circle: The Woman of Worth

The first major section of the Book of Proverbs, chapters 1–9, spoke of two women: Woman Folly (and the strange or foreign woman with whom she is symbolically identified) and Woman Wisdom. The final chapter of Proverbs, chapter 31, brings us full circle and closes the book by speaking of two women: the mother of Lemuel (verses 1–9) and the so-called capable wife or woman of valor (verses 10–31). Chapters 1–9 and 31 thus form a kind of thematic frame to the book. Having already considered Woman Wisdom in Proverbs 1–9, and having also already seen how Lemuel's mother instructs him in wisdom's way of social justice, we now consider more closely the "capable wife" or woman of "valor" or "worth" in Proverbs 31:10–31 and how this chapter sums up the themes the sages have been developing throughout the book.

> 10A capable wife who can find?
>   She is far more precious than jewels.
> 11The heart of her husband trusts in her,
>   and he will have no lack of gain.
> 12She does him good, and not harm,
>   all the days of her life.

¹³She seeks wool and flax,

   and works with willing hands.

¹⁴She is like the ships of the merchant,

   she brings her food from far away.

¹⁵She rises while it is still night

   and provides food for her household

   and tasks for her servant girls.

¹⁶She considers a field and buys it;

   with the fruit of her hands she plants a vineyard.

¹⁷She girds herself with strength,

   and makes her arms strong.

¹⁸She perceives that her merchandise is profitable.

   Her lamp does not go out at night.

¹⁹She puts her hands to the distaff,

   and her hands hold the spindle.

²⁰She opens her hand to the poor,

   and reaches out her hands to the needy.

²¹She is not afraid for her household when it snows,

   for all her household are clothed in crimson.

²²She makes herself coverings;

   her clothing is fine linen and purple.

²³Her husband is known in the city gates,

   taking his seat among the elders of the land.

²⁴She makes linen garments and sells them;

   she supplies the merchant with sashes.

²⁵Strength and dignity are her clothing,

   and she laughs at the time to come.

²⁶She opens her mouth with wisdom,

   and the teaching of kindness is on her tongue.

²⁷She looks well to the ways of her household,

   and does not eat the bread of idleness.

²⁸Her children rise up and call her happy;
 her husband too, and he praises her:
²⁹"Many women have done excellently,
 but you surpass them all."
³⁰Charm is deceitful, and beauty is vain,
 but a woman who fears the Lord is to be praised.
³¹Give her a share in the fruit of her hands,
 and let her works praise her in the city gates.
 (Proverbs 31:10–31; NRSV)

The ode to the woman of worth forms the final lines of the Book of Proverbs. Its artistry is revealed not only by its imagery and the way the sage-poet's words masterfully allude to other parts of Proverbs, but also by the fact that it takes the form of an acrostic, in which every stanza in the Hebrew text begins with a successive letter of the Hebrew alphabet. The phrase that in English is variously translated as "woman of worth," "woman of valor," "noble woman," or "capable wife" is *eshet hayil.* The Hebrew *hayil* is the adjective and carries a range of meanings, as the various translations "noble," "capable," and so on reflect. The figure in these lines is described as a potential wife to Proverbs' imagined male addressee, as the NRSV's translation of verse 10 makes clear. But given the range of possible translations for *eshet hayil,* it is also evident that rendering the phrase correctly into English in large part depends on whom or what, exactly, we think she is.

Scholars generally note three viable hypotheses when considering the identity of the *eshet hayil.* First, she may be imagined as the sort of real flesh-and-blood woman a young sage or student of wisdom might search for to be his bride, since the poem may reflect, more or less accurately, the roles and activities of at least some real women in the biblical period.[10] Second, she may reflect a kind of fantasy of the male writers of Proverbs as to what the perfect wife might be like, since the description of this woman, her roles and activities, is clearly presented as an ideal picture. Third, she may be a poetic representation or personification of the fundamental virtues of wisdom's way. That is, she may be Woman Wisdom herself, since the description of this woman mirrors the language used earlier in the book to describe wisdom.

Most likely, all three suggestions are partly right. The sages' description of the woman in Proverbs 31:10–31 is certainly based in part on the roles and activities that at least some women in the biblical period undertook. Yet the *eshet hayil* also represents the ancient, male sages' idealized, patriarchal vision of what a good wife should be like. Nonetheless, for a number of reasons we should also consider the *eshet hayil* fundamentally as a poetic representation of Woman Wisdom. She is described as constantly working (for example, verses 13, 19, 22), rising early (verse 15), as one who "does not eat the bread of idleness" (verse 27), and so on. The *eshet hayil* is thus diligent, a virtue that we have seen was so important to the sages throughout Proverbs. She likewise embodies another virtue central to the sages' vision of wisdom. She shows kindness to the poor, "opening her hand" and reaching out to the "needy" (verse 20).

The *eshet hayil,* finally, is also described in terms that are very close to the way the sages earlier described wisdom, both the virtue and its personification as a woman. In particular, the verses that speak of her by using images of money, riches, and poverty reflect precisely the sages' view on these matters as they appear elsewhere in the book. For instance, just as Woman Wisdom was described as "more precious than jewels" in Proverbs 3:15 (see p. 40), so verse 10 of the ode to the *eshet hayil* describes this woman in exactly the same way. Verse 11 also notes that her husband, or the one who finds or possesses her—the Hebrew for *husband* here is literally "possessor" (*ba'al*)—will not lack "gain." In Hebrew this word for "gain" is *sha-lal*, or "booty." It is one of the valuable things that the robbers offered the student of wisdom in Proverbs 1 in order to lure him onto the path of folly and wickedness. Now here, in the very last chapter of the book, the *eshet hayil* counters the robbers' initial offer and promises the one who will come to possess her, "her husband," the same valuable *shalal*.

In sum, just as Proverbs 1–9 presented Woman Wisdom as an attractive, marriageable woman, so here in chapter 31 the *eshet hayil* is presented as a desirable bride. The one who marries or possesses this woman—the one who follows the path of wisdom—will find something of great value. Proverbs' manner of describing wisdom as a woman whom men might possess will grate against our modern sensibilities and values. Indeed, the sages' message that wisdom is incomparably valuable ought not be uncritically passed on in the biased terms of the patriarchal past. When it came to equality of the genders, the sages, like many after them, failed to recognize the implications of their teachings about justice and equity. Yet by recognizing this today and asking how we ourselves might live up to the implications of the sages' teachings, which they themselves did not fully comprehend, we travel a step further down wisdom's way.

Final Reflections and Conclusions

The challenge that the Book of Proverbs sets before us as individuals, communities, and nations is to determine if we are living our lives in accord with wisdom's virtues and values. When it comes to questions of our money and wealth, in order to follow wisdom's way we need to measure ourselves against the standards or norms Proverbs holds out for us. For those of us of some means, living in the wealthiest country in the world, this means, in part, asking ourselves how "rich" we have become. Do we trust that our wealth can buy us security and well-being? Do we act honestly and fairly in our marketplaces of immense scale and complexity? Do we help the poor and marginalized in concrete ways? Do we genuinely hear their cries, or do we cover our ears by insisting to ourselves that our economic system and arrangements are the best we can do? Is our nation and are our communities looking out for the most economically and socially vulnerable in our midst? Or are the rules and laws set up to help those of us who are already well off? Our responses to all these money matters, the sages of Proverbs insist, have everything to do with the way of wisdom.

People of means ought never to forget the sages' insights regarding the threats to the life of wisdom that our wealth can bring. Although many of us may not believe ourselves to be "rich" in the negative moral sense that the sages used the term, our prosperity, Proverbs reminds us, inevitably puts us in a precarious position, morally speaking. When it comes to money and wealth, the sages teach that we are in a sense always prone to stray from wisdom's path of justice. Our prosperity is so desirable and so valuable that it may blind us to what we ought to do, whether by permitting us to turn a blind eye to the realities of the sources and costs of our prosperity, or by giving us the luxury of critiquing economic arrangements that we profit from without considering seriously how these might be reined in or reformed for the greater good. In short, our wealth can transform us into the "rich." To be wealthy or even a middle-class North American in the twenty-first century means, as theologian Darby Ray has written, "to enjoy unprecedented power and privilege."[11] It also means participating in social structures and economic systems whose "assumptions about human nature and the good life" are so broadly held that they are "nearly invisible." The sages ask us to place these assumptions in the clear light of day to see how they depart from the way of wisdom.

Because of the threats wealth presents, the sages' emphasis on social virtue must always be at the center of our concern—as it was for the sages themselves—when we consider whether or not we are traveling wisdom's way. The sages insist that we always ask first about the well-being of our communities, especially the poor and marginalized, and about our relationship to the establishment or destruction of that community—not about what benefits us most. At the same time, however, we ought not forget that the sages of Proverbs also ask us to use our intellectual gifts and to develop a practical wisdom when we consider how we might more fully travel the way of wisdom. They ask us to think about how we can transform our lives and communities so that they more fully correspond to wisdom's vision. This sort of concern, and acting on this concern, is actually a form of what many religious and spiritual traditions call "mercy," the compassionate treatment of others and the alleviating of their distress. Showing such mercy, however, is difficult for many of us today because, as the Latin American theologian Jon Sobrino has noted, "In this world we do not see 'mercy' regarded as a central value—there is more talk about 'freedom'—which means that 'the other' is not central, but 'myself.'"[12]

When we consider our money and Proverbs' way of wisdom, there is one other matter with which we ought, finally, to be concerned—namely, the antiquity and foreignness of the sages' teaching. As we said early on, Proverbs' wisdom comes to us across millennia and from a culture very different from ours, one that was quintessentially patriarchal and paternalistic. On the one hand, this means that for the sages, a woman's status, economic and otherwise, was dependent on that of the men in her life; first her father and subsequently her husband. The sages did not expect women to act independently in any social sphere, including the economic. On the other hand, it also means that the sages' response to poverty was to take care of the poor, as a father might take care of his children or other members of his family who could not take care of themselves. The sages' response to the poor was thus to give alms or act charitably in order to maintain them. It was not to consider how things might be fundamentally rearranged, or at least reformed, so that the poor would have a real opportunity to escape poverty and not simply be sustained in their poverty.

In this sense the sages, in part, failed to live up to the vision of justice implicit in their own writings, particularly those sayings that spoke of the fundamental equality of rich and poor, and, by extension, all humans (cf. Proverbs 22:2; 29:13 [p. 125]). However, by taking up in our own day the sages' invitation to embrace not only social virtue, but intellectual and practical virtues as well, we can and ought to consider how the *trajectory* of the sages' limited patriarchal and paternalistic vision of wisdom and justice might be extended forward for our world. Such a task, however, requires even more hard thinking about, for instance, the sorts of personal, communal, or national responses to the poor in our world. Do our responses to social inequality perpetuate the dependence of poor individuals, communities, and nations on their richer counterparts, almost guaranteeing that poor families and peoples remain in poverty? Or, do our responses reflect that underlying impulse toward equality that the sages haltingly gestured toward?

Proverbs 30:8–9 states:

> Give me neither poverty nor riches, but provide me with my daily bread, lest being sated, I renounce, saying "Who is the Lord?" Or, being impoverished, I take to theft and profane the name of my God. (NRSV)

According to some biblical commentators, this saying reveals that for the sages of Proverbs, the best life is the "middle class" life.[13] Yet besides erroneously suggesting that the ancient sages might have imagined anything like a North American middle-class lifestyle, such a view does not permit us to hear in these lines all the nuances of the sages' teachings about money and the way of wisdom that we have discovered in our exploration of Proverbs' path. Indeed, the verse can be said to sum up, or at least point toward, the range of Proverbs' teaching on wealth and poverty. The hope for neither poverty nor riches reminds us that the sages did not sanction the frenzied pursuit of wealth, and certainly not its attainment via unjust means. It reminds us that wealth is not the key to personal fulfillment or peace of mind; it is not what we ought to desire most. The verses underscore as well the dangers wealth poses to the life of wisdom. They note that the one who possesses wealth may, like a "rich" person, "renounce" the Lord and fail to acknowledge where true security and fullness of life lie—namely, in wisdom's way, in the intellectual, practical, and especially social virtues that the sages highlight. That the verses do not emphasize either riches or poverty likewise underscores that a minimum degree of economic well-being is necessary in order to live well and fully.

The sages don't glamorize poverty, but understand that it diminishes, and sometimes makes impossible, the fullness of life that all of God's creatures are entitled to enjoy. Although the lines don't explicitly point to our obligation to the poor and marginalized, the allusion to the precarious existence of the poor person, who might have to steal to survive, surely reminds us of that, too. In a very real way, then, the sages' desire for neither poverty nor riches, which Proverbs 30:8–9 points to, sums up Proverbs' teaching about money and the way of wisdom.

Dr. King noted that the arc of the moral universe was long, but bends toward justice. We said that this claim was similar to the claim that the Book of Proverbs makes about the universe being created by God "in wisdom." This image of a long arc bending toward justice helps us to understand that just as we today cannot see the end of the way of wisdom and justice, neither could the sages. Their formulation of wisdom and social justice, like ours, was inevitably partial, incomplete. What they truly offer us are foundational trajectories, which we ought not ignore, but which we ought to build on. We can do this because the sages of Proverbs also hoped that those, like us, who heard their instruction would live up to the social virtues as well as the practical and intellectual virtues they spoke of. When we take seriously the intellectual and practical contours of wisdom's way and discern where and how in our world and our lives the sages' teaching about money and riches might more fully be realized, we travel the way of wisdom.

My Path to *Money and the Way of Wisdom*

Money and the Way of Wisdom has grown out of my academic work on the Hebrew Book of Proverbs. In particular, some of the fundamental ideas that I put forth in these pages are developed and argued more rigorously in my *The Discourse of Wealth and Poverty in the Book of Proverbs*, Biblical Interpretation Series 77 (Leiden: E. J. Brill, 2006) and my "Revisiting the Prologue of Proverbs," *Journal of Biblical Literature*, 126, no. 3 (2007): 455–74. The entire journey began with a desire to create a relationship between my academic and intellectual interests and the real needs and problems of the world.

Money and the Way of Wisdom is primarily about what the Book of Proverbs has to say about wealth and poverty, the rich and the poor, justice and wisdom. But my broader concern is to present this material in a way that it might be useful to contemporary women and men. Because this is the case, throughout the book I inevitably speak about economics. I am, however, not an economist. Rather I have been trained in theology (MDiv, Princeton Theological Seminary) and as a professional and academic biblical scholar (PhD, Emory University). Hence whatever expertise I have in "money matters" lies not in the technical study of economics (far from it), but in evaluating the moral claims and outcomes of economic theories and policies and with presenting the economic and other values that biblical texts set forth.

In the interest of full disclosure to the reader, I should also say that in general I am convinced that any just economic arrangements must prioritize the well-being of the economically marginal. While recognizing the enormous complexity of contemporary economic arrangements and the competing ideologies of different schools of thought, I am largely persuaded by the arguments of economists such as Nobel Laureate Joseph Stiglitz who contend that current, dominant, global economic arrangements do not prioritize the poor, despite claims that such arrangements are the best path to widespread prosperity. Economists, policy makers, and others are involved in real and serious debate over whether and how such arrangements can be revolutionized or reformed to better serve the demands of justice for the poor. I do not believe a large-scale revolutionizing of the current system, to better serve the demands of justice to the poor, is likely to come about in the near future. Hence, for me, the reformist perspective of the likes of Stiglitz and others, which seeks to place some controls on global capitalism and recognizes this system's inability to attend to many of the demands of justice, are much preferable to the vision of the so-called market fundamentalists who largely reject such constraints and have significant faith in the ability of the market to rightly administer human life. For an intriguing theological perspective and analysis that appears to correspond broadly to the reformist perspective, see Kathryn Tanner, *Economy of Grace* (Minneapolis: Fortress Press, 2005).

Notes

Introduction

1. As reported by www.globalissues.org at www.globalissues.org/TradeRelated/Facts.asp (accessed August 27, 2008).

2. David R. Francis, "Why Higher Earners Work Longer Hours" at the National Bureau of Economic Research webpage at www.nber.org/digest/jul06/w11895.html (accessed August 27, 2008).

3. James Montier, "It Doesn't Pay: Materialism and the Pursuit of Happiness," as reported in a January 31, 2006, article in the *Times of London* by Carol Midgley entitled "Unhappy? That's Rich...," at www.timesonline.co.uk/tol/life_and_style/article723047.ece (accessed August 27, 2008).

4. As reported in an August 15, 2007, article of the *People's Daily Online*, entitled "People Unhappy with the Rich: Poll" at http://english.people.com.cn/90001/90776/90882/6240393.html (accessed August 27, 2008).

5. The *Economist,* vol. 381, no. 8509 (December 23, 2006): 13. The phenomenon of people in rich countries not enjoying a commensurate rise in happiness as their incomes have risen is sometimes referred to as the Easterlin paradox, for the researcher Richard A. Easterlin, who promoted this conclusion. See also the December 26, 2007, report in the *New York Times,* "Happiness for Sale," by Eduardo Porter, which reformulates the findings of the Easterlin paradox somewhat, though, in my view, hardly overturning the basic insight. See www.nytimes.com/2007/12/26/opinion/26wed4.html?_r=1&scp=1&sq=Easterlin+paradox&st=nyt&oref=slogin (accessed August 27, 2008).

6. Jennifer Michael Hecht, *The Happiness Myth: Why What We Think Is Right Is Wrong* (New York: HarperCollins, 2007), p. 175.

7. Martin Luther King Jr. "Where Do We Go from Here?" (Address to the Tenth Anniversary Convention of the Southern Christian Leadership Conference in Atlanta on August 16, 1967) in *A Testament to Hope: The Essential Writings and Speeches of Martin Luther King, Jr.*, edited by James Melvin Washington (San Francisco: HarperSanFrancisco, 1986), pp. 245–52, esp. p. 252.

8. *Maafa*, derived from a Kiswahili word, means "disaster" or "tragedy." *Shoah* is a Hebrew term that means "catastrophe."

9. King, "Where Do We Go from Here?" p. 252.

10. Timothy J. Sandoval, *The Discourse of Wealth and Poverty in the Book of Proverbs* (Leiden: E. J. Brill, 2006).

11. *The HarperCollins Study Bible: New Revised Standard Version* (New York: HarperCollins Publishers, 2006).

12. *Tanakh: The Holy Scriptures—The New JPS Translation According to the Traditional Hebrew Text* (Philadelphia, PA: Jewish Publication Society, 1985).

13. *Holy Bible, New International Version, NIV* (Grand Rapids, MI: Zondervan, 2002).

Chapter 1 "Proverbs" and the "Book" of Proverbs

1. A number of popular proverbs have been "translated" into more prosaic language. For example, consider the following: "You cannot estimate the value of the contents of a bound, printed narrative or record from its exterior vesture" ("You can't judge a book by its cover"). Other examples of this sort of "translation" of proverbs are widely available on the Internet. See for example, those posted by the webpage Grandma Faith at www3.telus.net/public/a7a55952/familiar- sayings.htm (accessed August 27, 2008).

2. My thinking regarding how language use might reflect real social struggles is influenced by the Russian literary theorist Mikhail Bakhtin. See, for example, *Problems of Dostoevsky's Poetics*, edited and translated by C. Emerson (Minneapolis: University of Minnesota Press, 1984).

3. See, for example, Ruth Finnegan, "Proverbs in Africa" in *The Wisdom of Many: Essays on the Proverb,* edited by Wolfgang Mieder and Alan Dundes (New York: Garland, 1981), pp. 389–418.

4. Wolfgang Mieder, "The Essence of Literary Proverb Study," *Proverbs* 23 (1974): 888–94, as reported by Carol R. Fontaine, *Traditional Sayings in the Old Testament* (Sheffield, UK: Almond Press, 1982), p. 54.

5. For in-depth discussions of how proverbs "work" or generate meaning, see George Lakoff and Mark Turner, *More Than Cool Reason: A Field Guide to Poetic Metaphor* (Chicago: University of Chicago Press, 1989) and Peter Seitel, "Proverbs: A Social Use of Metaphor" in *The Wisdom of Many: Essays on the Proverb* (Madison: University of Wisconsin Press), pp. 126–38.

6. Diane Bergant, *Israel's Wisdom Literature: A Liberation-Critical Reading* (Minneapolis: Fortress, 1997). Other scholars make similar arguments. Cf. Tremper Longman III, *Proverbs* (Grand Rapids, MI: Baker Academic, 2006).

7. For a helpful overview of the larger scholarly discussion about the nature and origin of the sayings in the book of Proverbs, see "The Social Location of the Book of Proverbs" in *Texts, Temples, and Traditions: A Tribute to Menahem Haran,* edited by Michael V. Fox, Victor Avigdor Hurowitz, Avi Hurvitz, Michael L. Klein, Baruch J. Schwartz, Nili Shupak (Winona Lake, IN: Eisenbrauns, 1996), pp. 227–39.

8. The editor of the collection in which the Igbo saying is recorded similarly explains that the proverb can be used to express the idea that alcohol "enables people to do things in their imagination that they would never have attempted in reality." *Proverbs of Africa: Human Nature in the Nigerian Oral Tradition,* edited by Ryszard Pachocinski (St. Paul, MN: PWPA, 1996).

9. Cf., for example, the perspective of Michael V. Fox in his excellent commentary, *Proverbs 1–9: A New Translation with Introduction and Commentary,* Anchor Bible 18a (New York: Doubleday, 2000).

Chapter 2 Understanding the Book of Proverbs

1. For more on the strange/foreign woman and Woman Wisdom, see Claudia V. Camp, *Wise, Strange and Holy: The Strange Woman and the Making of the Bible* (Sheffield, UK: Sheffield Academic Press, 2000) and Christine Roy Yoder, *Wisdom as a Woman of Substance: A Socioeconomic Reading of Proverbs 1–9 and 31:10–31* (Berlin: Walter de Gruyter, 2001).

2. For a more in-depth argument, see Timothy J. Sandoval, "Revisiting the Prologue of Proverbs," *Journal of Biblical Literature,* 126, no. 3 (2007): 455–73.

3. As with other biblical books, in the Jewish tradition the first word of Proverbs forms the Hebrew title of the book—*Mishle. Mishle* is followed immediately by the name *Shlomo* (Solomon) and the two together mean "The Proverbs of Solomon."

4. See Sandoval, *Discourse*, p. 213.

5. Among many verses, cf. Amos 5:24; Isaiah 1:27; Micah 3:1.

6. Cf., for example, Ezekiel 17:2 and 24:3; Judges 14:12–19; Habakkuk 2:6.

7. Cf. Sandoval, "Revisiting the Prologue."

8. In the ancient Near East, sometimes wisdom "teachers" were figuratively called "fathers," and "pupils" were referred to as "sons." The designations may reflect the origin of ancient schools in the household. On the vexing question of the presence of schools in ancient Israel, see James L. Crenshaw, *Education in Ancient Israel: Across the Deadening Silence* (New York: Doubleday, 1998).

9. Alice Calaprice, ed., *The Expanded Quotable Einstein* (Princeton, NJ: Princeton University Press, 2000), p. 292.

10. As reported by the Organic Consumers Organization at http://www.organicconsumers.org/articles/article_4738.cfm (accessed August 27, 2008).

11. Ibid.

12. This is true even when one accounts for differences in education and experience that might result in initial lower wages for some women and minorities. According to 2006 U.S. Census data, as reported by the Pearson Education run webpage www.infoplease.com, white women continue to earn about three-fourths what white men earn, African-American women, about 64 percent, and Hispanic women just over half. See www.infoplease.com/us/census/median-earnings-by-race-2006.html (accessed August 27, 2008).

13. Joseph E. Stiglitz, *Globalization and Its Discontents* (New York: W. W. Norton and Company, 2002), p. 52.

14. George Soros, *On Globalization* (New York: PublicAffairs, 2002), p. 5.

15. As quoted at www.katinkahesselink.net/tibet/dalai-lama-quotes.html (accessed August 27, 2008).

16. See further the work by Yoder, *Wisdom as a Woman of Substance.*

17. For more on John Wesley and money, see Theodore W. Jennings Jr., *Good News to the Poor: John Wesley's Evangelical Economics* (Nashville: Abingdon, 1990).

18. As cited by www.catholictradition.org at www.catholictradition.org/Saints/saintly-quotes.htm (accessed August 27, 2008).

19. The one exception is Proverbs 3:9, which uses the same term for wealth, but in the context of exhorting the original readers to faithfully hand over their gifts or tithes to the Lord at the Temple.

20. Although a few scholars go to great lengths to argue that *tzedekah* in this instance can rightly be rendered as "success" or "prosperity," the majority of contemporary commentators understand that it should be translated as "righteousness" or "justice," even if they do not recognize that a significant interpretive issue is at stake. Interestingly, of the modern English translations that I've consulted, only the old rendering of the King James Version translates *tzedekah* as "righteousness."

21. Jon Sobrino, *Where Is God? Earthquake, Terrorism, Barbarity, and Hope* (Maryknoll, NY: Orbis Books, 2004), 19; italics original.

Chapter 3 Wisdom's Virtues in the Book of Proverbs

1. See the March 1, 2005, *Washington Post* article by Blaine Harden entitled, "Utility Exposes Enron Greed at its Core" at www.washingtonpost.com/wp-dyn/articles/A61253-2005Feb28.html (accessed August 27, 2008).

2. See the March 10, 2008, article in *InvestmentNews* by Jeff Benjamin entitled, "Assets jump 18% in socially conscious investments" at www.investmentnews.com/apps/pbcs.dll/article?AID=/20080310/REG/782570549 (accessed August 27, 2008).

3. Martin Luther King Jr., *The Strength to Love* (New York: Harper and Row, 1963), p. 51.

4. Rabbi Irving Greenberg, *The Jewish Way: Living the Holidays* (New York: Touchstone, 1988), p. 135.

5. *The Expanded Quotable Einstein,* p. 305.

6. Other sayings in Proverbs that are concerned with right speech include: 12:17; 14:5, 25; 19:5, 9, 28; 21:28; 24:26, 28; 25:9, 18. Cf. further 12:22; 17:15; 18:5; 24:24; 28:21.

7. As reported in Alex Ayres, ed., *The Wisdom of Martin Luther King, Jr.* (New York: Meridian, 1993), p. 108.

8. Jürgen Moltmann, *The Source of Life: The Holy Spirit and the Theology of Life* (Minneapolis: Fortress, 1997), p. 109.

9. See the January 27, 2008, article in the *New York Times* by Mark Bittman entitled, "Rethinking the Meat Guzzler." See www.nytimes.com/2008/01/27/weekinreview/ 27bittman.html?_r=1&scp=2&sq=meat+consumption&st=nyt&oref= login (accessed August 27, 2008).

10. See the January 19, 2006, article in the *San Francisco Chronicle* by Cyril Penn entitled "US wine consumption keeps going up" at www.sfgate.com/cgi-bin/article.cgi?f=/c/a/2006/01/19/WIGJGGOS9V1.DTL (accessed August 27, 2008).

11. See the *New York Times* Archives at http://query.nytimes.com/gst/abstract.html?res=9904E4D8103AEF34BC4E51DFBF66838C679FDE (accessed August 27, 2008).

12. As cited by QuotesandPoems.com, http://www.quotesandpoem.com/quotes/listquotes/author/albert-schweitzer (accessed August 27, 2008).

13. See the information provided by the Bill and Melinda Gates Foundation at www.gatesfoundation.org/MediaCenter/FactSheet/ (accessed August 27, 2008).

14. Adam Smith, *The Wealth of Nations* (New York: Modern Library, 1985); originally published in 1776.

15. Stiglitz, *Globalization,* p. 78.

16. Soros, *On Globalization,* p. 7.

17. See http://www.msnbc.msn.com/id/17803920/ (accessed August 27, 2008).

18. John Cavanagh and Jerry Mander, eds., *Alternatives to Economic Globalization: A Better World Is Possible* (San Francisco: Berrett-Koehler, 2002).

19. Cf. Proverbs 24:33–34.

Chapter 4 Social Justice in the Book of Proverbs

1. The data for the United States is according to the U.S. Census Bureau, as reported by N. C. Aizenman and Christopher Lee in "U.S. Poverty Rate Drops; Ranks of Uninsured Grow," *Washington Post* (August 29, 2007). See www.washingtonpost.com/wp-dyn/content/ article/2007/08/28/AR2007082800779.html (accessed August 27, 2008). For global statistics, cf. http://www.globalissues.org/TradeRelated/Facts.asp (accessed August 27, 2008), and Introduction, n. 1.

2. For an account of the economic context for the preaching of Isaiah (and other Israelite prophets of his time), including the oppressive measures enacted by political and economic elites, see Marvin L. Chaney, "Bitter Bounty: The Dynamics of Political Economy Critiqued by the Eighth-Century Prophets" in *Reformed Faith and Economics,* edited by R. Stivers (Lanham, MD: University Press of America, 1989), pp. 15–30, and the book-length work of Chaney's student, D. N. Premnath, *Eighth Century Prophets: A Social Analysis* (St. Louis: Chalice Press, 2003).

3. See, for instance, Deuteronomy. 10:17–18; 24:17.

4. My rendering of these lines draws not only on the NRSV, but on the translation work of Tremper Longman III in his commentary *Proverbs* (Grand Rapids, MI: Baker Academic, 2006), pp. 425–26.

5. See the information provided by the National Runaway Switchboard at www.1800runaway.org/ (accessed August 27, 2008).

6. See U.S. State Department report at https://usinfo.state.gov/gi/global_ issues/human_trafficking.html (accessed August 27, 2008) and the Catholic Bishops' position paper at http://www.usccb.org/mrs/traffick-ingweb.shtml (accessed August 27, 2008).

7. See Covenant House at http://www.covenanthouse.org/index.html (accessed August 27, 2008).

8. Although the Hebrew of this verse is equivocal, other scholars suggest that the "ruler" in question is a political figure. Cf., for instance, the comments of Longman, *Proverbs,* pp. 492–93.

9. In a unique twist, Lemuel's mother also advises the future king to provide the destitute with "strong drink" in order that they might "forget their poverty" and "remember their poverty no more" (NRSV). I know of no other similar exhortations in the ancient Near East.

10. The translation is Longman's. See *Proverbs,* p. 502.

11. The translation is Longman's. See ibid., p. 510. Cf. further the difficult Proverbs 16:10, which speaks of a king's "oracular" activity, but also notes that the king "does not betray justice with his mouth." p. 331.

12. See John Witte Jr., *Religion and the American Constitutional Experiment: Essential Rights and Liberties* (Boulder, CO: Westview Press, 2000), esp. pp. 231–39, and Jeffrey Stout, *Democracy and Tradition* (Princeton, NJ: Princeton University Press, 2004).

13. See my entry "Balances" in the *Encyclopedia of the Bible and Its Reception,* edited by H. Spieckermann and C. L. Seow (Berlin: Walter DeGruyter, forthcoming).

14. My translation of this passage is indebted to the work of Fox, *Proverbs 1–9,* p. 210.

15. For a fuller and more technical argument for my interpretation of this passage, see *Discourse,* pp. 107–112.

16. Cf. Proverbs 27:13.

17. Cf. Fox, *Proverbs* 1–9, p. 215.

18. As reported in the April 5, 2008, *New York Times* article by Elizabeth Malkin entitled "Microfinance's Success Sets Off a Debate in Mexico" at www.nytimes.com/2008/04/05/business/worldbusiness/05micro.html?s cp=1&sq=compartamos&st=nyt (accessed August 27, 2008).

19. See the February 16, 2004, report by congressman George Miller for the Democratic Staff of the Committee on Education and the Workforce of the U.S. House of Representatives entitled, "Everyday Low Wages: The Hidden Price We All Pay for Wal-Mart." The report is available through www.mindfully.org at www.mindfully.org/Industry/ 2004/Wal-Mart-Labor-Record16feb04.htm (accessed August 27, 2008).

20. See the August 26, 2002, article in *Forbes* by Penelope Patsuris entitled, "The Corporate Scandal Sheet" at www.forbes.com/2002/ 07/25/accountingtracker.html (accessed August 27, 2008).

21. See the Students Organizing for Labor and Economic Equality web page at www.umich.edu/~sole/sffaq.html (accessed August 27, 2008).

22. As quoted at www.heartquotes.net/Einstein.html (accessed August 27, 2008).

Chapter 5 Discerning Wisdom and the Woman of Worth

1. Cf. Michael V. Fox, "The Epistemology of the Book of Proverbs," *Journal of Biblical Literature,* 126, no. 4 (2007): 669–84, esp. 670–74.

2. See, for example, the list of authors cited in Sandoval, *Discourse,* p. 31, note 11.

3. See, for instance, the work of Jubilee USA Network at www.jubileeusa. org/ (accessed August 27, 2008).

4. See the September 8, 1988, article in the *New York Times* by Stephen Labaton entitled "Drexel Burnham Charged by S.E.C. with Stock Fraud" at http://query.nytimes.com/gst/fullpage.html?res= 940DE1DE163DF93BA3575AC0A96E948260 (accessed August 27,

2008) and Labaton's December 22, 1988, *New York Times* article entitled "Drexel Concedes Guilt on Trading; to Pay $650 Million" at http://query.nytimes.com/gst/fullpage.html?res=940DE3D9133EF931A 15751C1A96E948260 (accessed August 27, 2008). Milken and his defenders continue to maintain his innocence. See www.mikemilken.com (accessed August 27, 2008).

5. Sandoval, *Discourse,* p. 196.

6. The proverb continues in the NRSV rendering, "Do not go to the house of your kindred in the day of your calamity. Better is a neighbor who is nearby than kindred who are far away." Especially the middle portion of 27:10 may be a secondary addition. For further discussion, see Sandoval, *Discourse,* p. 196–98.

7. See, especially, Walter C. Kaiser Jr., "The Old Testament Promise of Material Blessings and the Contemporary Believer," *Trinity Journal,* 9 (1988): 151–70. Cf., too, J. David Pleins, "Poverty in the Social World of the Wise," *Journal for the Study of the Old Testament,* 37 (1987): 61-78.

8. See the July 1, 1996, *New York Times* article by Ronald Smothers entitled, "As Olympics Approach, Homeless Are Not Feeling at Home in Atlanta" at http://query.nytimes.com/gst/fullpage.html?res= 990DE7DB1E39F932A35754C0A960958260&sec=&spon=&page-wanted=2 (accessed August 27, 2008).

9. The Sam Walton story is widely known. See, for example www.usdreams. com/WaltonW35.html (accessed August 27, 2008) and the account by Joshua Kennon at http://beginnersinvest.about.com/od/samwalton/p/ aasamwalton.htm (accessed August 27, 2008).

10. On the *eshet hayil,* see again Yoder, *Wisdom as a Woman of Substance.* Cf. further Camp, *Wise, Strange and Holy.*

11. Darby Ray, "Tracking the Tragic: Augustine, Global Capitalism, and a Theology of Struggle" in *Constructive Theology: A Contemporary Approach to Classical Themes,* edited by Serene Jones and Paul Lakeland (Minneapolis: Fortress Press, 2005), 135.

12. See Sobrino, *Where Is God: Earthquake, Terrorism, Barbarity and Hope* (Maryknoll, NY: Orbis, 2004), p. xxix.

13. Cf. Longman, *Proverbs,* pp. 524–25.

DISCUSSION GUIDE

Chapter 1

～ What proverbs did your grandparents or parents (or others) use to caution you when you were younger? What wisdom did you learn from these proverbs? Do you use these proverbs with your children (or with other people)? Why or why not?

～ Think about some of the expressions you use every day. Can you recognize any proverbs in your daily speech?

Chapter 2

～ What or who do you think of when you hear the word *justice*? Do you think of a court room? An eye for an eye?

～ What do you think of when you hear the word *righteousness*? Do you think of piety? Good behavior?

～ Why do you think these images or concepts come to mind?

～ Given the Prologue's emphasis on social virtue (see pp. 23–27), what sorts of attitudes and behaviors do you imagine the sages of Proverbs will associate with the way of wisdom and the way of folly when it comes to money and economics?

~ In what ways or for what reasons do people you know, or people you have heard about, attempt to pursue money "at all costs" like the robbers in Proverbs 1 (see pp. 27–30)?

~ What aspects of your life (the clothes you buy, the coffee you drink) might you investigate to discover if these are enjoyed at a high costs to others, perhaps half a world a way?

~ How might you begin to change these parts of your life so that they are more in accord with wisdom's way?

~ In what ways might you, or people you know, be sacrificing a happier existence by an endless pursuit to acquire "just a little bit more"?

~ What "things" do you have more than enough of, but nonetheless continually desire more and more of? (Shoes? Certain foods? Electronics? Books?).

~ For you, what is more precious than money? (Family? Friends? Your faith community? Baseball?) Why?

~ Which of your possessions would you be willing to give up in order to acquire (or "buy") the peace of mind, contentment, security, and justice toward which the sages claim the way of wisdom leads? What would you never give up? Why?

~ Why do you think the sages of Proverbs believe that wisdom's virtues—especially social virtues like social justice—are the most valuable thing you might ever acquire? How or why do you imagine things like social justice to be valuable—for you personally, for your communities?

Chapter 3

~ When you think about how the "proverbs" of Proverbs might help you view the specific contours of wisdom's path when it comes to money and economics, what sorts of questions are you hoping the sages will answer? (How should I spend my money? How can I make the most money possible? How much of my money should I give away? What are the best business practices or strategies? How can I get out of debt? Should the government help the poor and if so, how?)

~ What specific adjustments in your attitude toward, or use of, your money might you make to let your economic life be more fully guided by the wisdom the sages believed is structured into the cosmos?

~ In your view, is there a difference between prospering economically and enjoying a "good life"? How would you describe that difference?

~ Do you need to have money to enjoy a good life? How might too much money make enjoying a good life difficult or impossible?

~ Do you agree with the interpretation of the sages' teaching that the possession of much money always presents a danger to living a moral life?

~ Is Einstein correct that money always "tempts its owner to abuse it"? Why or Why not?

~ Who do you believe are the prophets of our day whose words, though they may be bothersome and even offensive to some, might nonetheless over time prove to be what the sages understood as the "right speech" that promotes justice?

~ What are the virtues that best describe the religious, civic, or other sort of community (club, university) with which you are most actively or intimately involved? How are you "richer" for being a part of that community?

~ What specifically might you name as your "rich" vices? What are
the "rich" vices of your faith community, your nation? How might
you transform those vices, or begin to help your community or
nation transform their vices into wise virtues like generosity and
social justice?

~ The sages did not think laziness "causes" poverty or that diligence
"causes" wealth. Do you agree? Why? If you disagree with the
sages, how might you imagine trying to convince the sages of
your point of view? How do you imagine they might respond to
your objections?

Chapter 4

~ What are some specific ways that you already, or might start to,
show kindness to the poor? What motivates you to engage in this
sort of charity?

~ Do you believe your "kindness to the poor" makes a real difference (or enough of a difference) for the disadvantaged of the
world? If not, what do you think would have to happen for such
a real difference to come about?

~ How do you see the rights of the poor abused today?

~ Do you agree with the ancient sages that our individual and collective
economic decisions today ought to be evaluated in light of whether
they result in more justice for the poor and needy of our world?

~ What sorts of concrete steps might you take toward making this
vision a reality?

~ Besides the economically poor, who else today lives on the margins of
our communities and society? How might you and others attempt to
begin to include these people into your community or society?

~ The sages taught that governments should assist the poor in their realm. How does this affirm or challenge your own political values?

~ How do you imagine that showing kindness to the poor in the sages' day would be different than showing kindness to the poor today?

~ In light of these differences, how might you "translate" the sages' moral demand, that kings attend to the most vulnerable in their realms, for the world you live in?

~ What sorts of markets do you participate in regularly? (Supermarkets? Stock markets? Others?)

~ If you don't use balances and weights in your daily transactions, what practices might you equate with the use of false balances and weights in the ancient markets?

~ Do you regularly lend money to others or borrow money to purchase items you desire? (don't forget to think about credit card debt) Has your experience in this regard been good or bad? Why was it good or bad?

~ If you have ever borrowed or loaned money, what was your motivation for doing so? Is it something that you imagine sages like Sirach would have approved of (like helping out a friend in hard times)?

~ What are some ways the ancient sages' wisdom about borrowing and lending might be transferred to your life?

~ What is the difference between a bribe and a gift?

~ Why do most people today not approve of the giving and taking of bribes but have no problem with gift giving? How do these contemporary attitudes compare with the sages' understanding of when a bribe or gift belongs to folly's way?

Chapter 5

~ If the ancient sages were to ask you directly what you were willing to do so that wisdom's justice might be more fully present in your life and community and in society at large, how would you respond? Make a list of possible actions (from learning more about local labor struggles and the effects of free trade on the poorest people of the world, to lobbying your representatives in support of legislation that bends toward wisdom's justice, to buying fair trade products).

~ Reread Proverbs 13:8 (p. 118), Proverbs 18:23 (p. 121), and Proverbs 22:7 (p. 121). For each verse try to imagine a situation from your life today that illustrates the truth of these proverbs.

~ What are some examples from our world of how wealth is a "fortress" for the rich and poverty a person's "ruin," as Proverbs 10:15 (p. 117) puts it?

~ Can you think of examples from your own life, or the life of people you know, that illustrate the truth of sayings like Proverbs 14:20; 19:4; 19:6 and 19:7 (pp. 122–123)?

~ If the sages of Proverbs are correct, and relationships that primarily revolve around a person's money are often weak, why do you think this is so? In your view, what is the best foundation for solid relationships—both close personal relationships and those less intimate relationships with others in our communities and society?

~ The sages affirmed the fundamental equality of humans because God creates all. They recognized, however, that the poor were often not treated with equality, but were exploited as second-class citizens. Who in your community or in the world today is discriminated against because of their economic status, or for any other reason? Do you see any connection between economic status and the other reasons for discrimination? How might unjust or discriminatory relationships in your community be transformed by using the wisdom of the sages?

~ Who are the people you know who, though they do not possess a lot of money, are rich in virtue or wisdom? How did they attain this great "wealth"?

~ Reread Proverbs 22:16 (p. 129). Thinking about the sages' emphasis on social virtue (the value of community), justice (showing kindness to the poor), and the "rich" (as morally suspect), can you imagine situations today where that verse may be apt?

~ The virtues that the *eshet hayil* possesses are largely those that belong to wisdom's way. Having thus come full circle in our study, what aspects of wisdom's teaching about wealth and poverty are most important to you?

~ Which virtues and what values do you hope to make more fully a part of your life?

~ What two or three concrete or specific steps will you take to make this a reality?

SUGGESTIONS FOR FURTHER READING

General Study of Proverbs

Mieder, Wolfgang. *Proverbs Are Never Out of Season: Popular Wisdom in the Modern Age.* Oxford, UK: Oxford University Press, 1993.

Collections of Proverbs and Wise Sayings

Ayres, Alex, ed., *The Wisdom of Martin Luther King, Jr.: An A-to-Z Guide to the Ideas and Ideals of the Great Civil Rights Leader.* New York: Meridian, 1993.

Ballesteros, Octavio A., ed. *Mexican Proverbs: The Philosophy, Wisdom and Humor of a People.* Waco, TX: Eakin Press, 1980.

Calaprice, Alice, ed. *The Expanded Quotable Einstein.* Princeton, NJ: Princeton University Press, 2000.

Gross, David C., ed. *Dictionary of 1,000 Jewish Proverbs.* New York: Hippocrene, 1993.

Olivelle, Patrick, trans. *Pancatantra: The Book of India's Folk Wisdom.* Oxford, UK: Oxford University Press, 1997.

Pachocinski, Ryszard, ed. *Proverbs of Africa: Human Nature in the Nigerian Oral Tradition.* St. Paul, MN: PWPA, 1996.

Prahlad, Sw. Anand, ed. *African American Proverbs in Context*. Jackson: University Press of Mississippi, 1996.

Ward, Benedicta, ed. *The Sayings of the Desert Fathers*. Oxford, UK: A. R. Mowbray, 1975.

Scholarly Commentaries on the Book of Proverbs

Fox, Michael V. *Proverbs 1–9: A New Translation with Introduction and Commentary*. Anchor Bible 18a. New York: Doubleday, 2000.

Longman, Tremper, III. *Proverbs*. Grand Rapids, MI: Baker Academic, 2006.

On Biblical Wisdom Literature

Bergant, Diane. *Israel's Wisdom Literature: A Liberation-Critical Reading*. Minneapolis: Fortress, 1997.

Murphy, Roland E. *The Tree of Life: An Exploration of Biblical Wisdom Literature*. Grand Rapids, MI: Eerdmans, 2002.

Shapiro, Rami. *The Divine Feminine in Biblical Wisdom Literature: Selections Annotated & Explained*. Woodstock, VT: SkyLight Paths, 2005.

ACKNOWLEDGMENTS

I am grateful to Maura Shaw, formerly of SkyLight Paths, for approaching me with the idea for this book and especially to project editor Mark Ogilbee (also now formerly of SkyLight Paths), who took over the project and guided it essentially to its conclusion. In particular, I am deeply grateful for Mark's countless suggestions, kind prodding, and elegant prose, of which I have availed myself many times in this volume. For many of the finer turns of phrase that appear in these pages, Mark deserves credit. The book is incomparably richer and better written because of Mark's assistance. Emily Wichland, vice president of Editorial and Production, and Heidi White, assistant editor, have gracefully seen the book through the final publication process, for which I am also grateful.

Thanks are also due to my many students at the Chicago Theological Seminary who have challenged me to better develop my ideas about money, wealth, and poverty, and the Book of Proverbs. A good bit of the material in this book was developed in a course I have taught in years past called "Wisdom, Wealth, and Poverty." For the support of my friends and colleagues in Chicago and beyond, I am also grateful. My wife Maria Antonieta also deserves my special thanks for her love and encouragement in all my work. The book is dedicated to her parents, who, though not wealthy by the measures of this world, are rich in wisdom and virtue.

INDEX OF VERSES

Other Verses

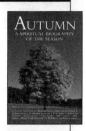

Sacred Texts—SkyLight Illuminations Series

Offers today's spiritual seeker an accessible entry into the great classic texts of the world's spiritual traditions. Each classic is presented in an accessible translation, with facing pages of guided commentary from experts, giving you the keys you need to understand the history, context and meaning of the text. This series enables you, whatever your background, to experience and understand classic spiritual texts directly, and to make them a part of your life.

CHRISTIANITY

The End of Days: Essential Selections from Apocalyptic Texts—
Annotated & Explained *Annotation by Robert G. Clouse*
Helps you understand the complex Christian visions of the end of the world.
5½ x 8½, 224 pp, Quality PB, 978-1-59473-170-9 **$16.99**

The Hidden Gospel of Matthew: Annotated & Explained
Translation & Annotation by Ron Miller
Takes you deep into the text cherished around the world to discover the words and events that have the strongest connection to the historical Jesus.
5½ x 8½, 272 pp, Quality PB, 978-1-59473-038-2 **$16.99**

The Lost Sayings of Jesus: Teachings from Ancient Christian, Jewish, Gnostic and Islamic Sources—Annotated & Explained
Translation & Annotation by Andrew Phillip Smith; Foreword by Stephan A. Hoeller
This collection of more than three hundred sayings depicts Jesus as a Wisdom teacher who speaks to people of all faiths as a mystic and spiritual master.
5½ x 8½, 240 pp, Quality PB, 978-1-59473-172-3 **$16.99**

Philokalia: The Eastern Christian Spiritual Texts—Selections Annotated & Explained *Annotation by Allyne Smith; Translation by G. E. H. Palmer, Phillip Sherrard and Bishop Kallistos Ware*
The first approachable introduction to the wisdom of the Philokalia, which is the classic text of Eastern Christian spirituality.
5½ x 8½, 240 pp, Quality PB, 978-1-59473-103-7 **$16.99**

The Sacred Writings of Paul: Selections Annotated & Explained
Translation & Annotation by Ron Miller
Explores the apostle Paul's core message of spiritual equality, freedom and joy.
5½ x 8½, 224 pp, Quality PB, 978-1-59473-213-3 **$16.99**

Sex Texts from the Bible: Selections Annotated & Explained
Translation & Annotation by Teresa J. Hornsby; Foreword by Amy-Jill Levine
Offers surprising insight into our modern sexual lives.
5½ x 8½, 208 pp, Quality PB, 978-1-59473-217-1 **$16.99**

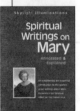

Spiritual Writings on Mary: Annotated & Explained
Annotation by Mary Ford-Grabowsky; Foreword by Andrew Harvey
Examines the role of Mary, the mother of Jesus, as a source of inspiration in history and in life today. 5½ x 8½, 288 pp, Quality PB, 978-1-59473-001-6 **$16.99**

The Way of a Pilgrim: The Jesus Prayer Journey—Annotated & Explained
Translation & Annotation by Gleb Pokrovsky; Foreword by Andrew Harvey
This classic of Russian spirituality is the delightful account of one man who sets out to learn the prayer of the heart, also known as the "Jesus prayer."
5½ x 8½, 160 pp, Illus., Quality PB, 978-1-893361-31-7 **$14.95**

Sacred Texts—cont.

MORMONISM

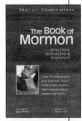

The Book of Mormon: Selections Annotated & Explained
Annotation by Jana Riess; Foreword by Phyllis Tickle
Explores the sacred epic that is cherished by more than twelve million members
of the LDS church as the keystone of their faith.
5½ x 8½, 272 pp, Quality PB, 978-1-59473-076-4 **$16.99**

NATIVE AMERICAN

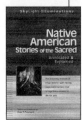

Native American Stories of the Sacred: Annotated & Explained
Retold & Annotated by Evan T. Pritchard
Intended for more than entertainment, these teaching tales contain elegantly simple illustrations of time-honored truths.
5½ x 8½, 272 pp, Quality PB, 978-1-59473-112-9 **$16.99**

GNOSTICISM

Gnostic Writings on the Soul: Annotated & Explained
Translation & Annotation by Andrew Phillip Smith; Foreword by Stephan A. Hoeller
Reveals the inspiring ways your soul can remember and return to its unique,
divine purpose.
5½ x 8½, 144 pp, Quality PB, 978-1-59473-220-1 **$16.99**

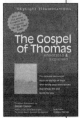

The Gospel of Philip: Annotated & Explained
Translation & Annotation by Andrew Phillip Smith; Foreword by Stevan Davies
Reveals otherwise unrecorded sayings of Jesus and fragments of Gnostic mythology.
5½ x 8½, 160 pp, Quality PB, 978-1-59473-111-2 **$16.99**

The Gospel of Thomas: Annotated & Explained
Translation & Annotation by Stevan Davies Sheds new light on the origins of Christianity and
portrays Jesus as a wisdom-loving sage.
5½ x 8½, 192 pp, Quality PB, 978-1-893361-45-4 **$16.99**

The Secret Book of John: The Gnostic Gospel—Annotated & Explained
Translation & Annotation by Stevan Davies The most significant and influential text of
the ancient Gnostic religion.
5½ x 8½, 208 pp, Quality PB, 978-1-59473-082-5 **$16.99**

JUDAISM

The Divine Feminine in Biblical Wisdom Literature
Selections Annotated & Explained
Translation & Annotation by Rabbi Rami Shapiro; Foreword by Rev. Cynthia Bourgeault, PhD
Uses the Hebrew books of Psalms, Proverbs, Song of Songs, Ecclesiastes and Job,
Wisdom literature and the Wisdom of Solomon to clarify who Wisdom is.
5½ x 8½, 240 pp, Quality PB, 978-1-59473-109-9 **$16.99**

Ethics of the Sages: *Pirke Avot*—Annotated & Explained
Translation & Annotation by Rabbi Rami Shapiro Clarifies the ethical teachings of the
early Rabbis. 5½ x 8½, 192 pp, Quality PB, 978-1-59473-207-2 **$16.99**

Hasidic Tales: Annotated & Explained
Translation & Annotation by Rabbi Rami Shapiro
Introduces the legendary tales of the impassioned Hasidic rabbis, presenting them as
stories rather than as parables. 5½ x 8½, 240 pp, Quality PB, 978-1-893361-86-7 **$16.95**

The Hebrew Prophets: Selections Annotated & Explained
Translation & Annotation by Rabbi Rami Shapiro; Foreword by Zalman M. Schachter-Shalomi
Focuses on the central themes covered by all the Hebrew prophets.
5½ x 8½, 224 pp, Quality PB, 978-1-59473-037-5 **$16.99**

Zohar: Annotated & Explained *Translation & Annotation by Daniel C. Matt*
The best-selling author of *The Essential Kabbalah* brings together in one place the most
important teachings of the Zohar, the canonical text of Jewish mystical tradition.
5½ x 8½, 176 pp, Quality PB, 978-1-893361-51-5 **$15.99**

Spirituality

Next to Godliness: Finding the Sacred in Housekeeping
Edited and with Introductions by Alice Peck
Offers new perspectives on how we can reach out for the Divine.
6 x 9, 224 pp, Quality PB, 978-1-59473-214-0 **$19.99**

Bread, Body, Spirit: Finding the Sacred in Food
Edited and with Introductions by Alice Peck
Explores how food feeds our faith. 6 x 9, 224 pp, Quality PB, 978-1-59473-242-3 **$19.99**

Renewal in the Wilderness: A Spiritual Guide to Connecting with God
in the Natural World *by John Lionberger*
Reveals the power of experiencing God's presence in many variations of the natural world. 6 x 9, 176 pp, b/w photos, Quality PB, 978-1-59473-219-5 **$16.99**

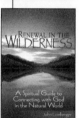

Honoring Motherhood: Prayers, Ceremonies and Blessings
Edited and with Introductions by Lynn L. Caruso
Journey through the seasons of motherhood. 5 x 7¼, 272 pp, HC, 978-1-59473-239-3 **$19.99**

Soul Fire: Accessing Your Creativity *by Rev. Thomas Ryan, CSP*
Learn to cultivate your creative spirit. 6 x 9, 160 pp, Quality PB, 978-1-59473-243-0 **$16.99**

Technology & Spirituality: How the Information Revolution Affects
Our Spiritual Lives *by Stephen K. Spyker* 6 x 9, 176 pp, HC, 978-1-59473-218-8 **$19.99**

Money and the Way of Wisdom: Insights from the Book of Proverbs
by Timothy J. Sandoval, PhD 6 x 9, 192 pp (est), Quality PB, 978-1-59473-245-4 **$16.99**

Awakening the Spirit, Inspiring the Soul
30 Stories of Interspiritual Discovery in the Community of Faiths
Edited by Brother Wayne Teasdale and Martha Howard, MD; Foreword by Joan Borysenko, PhD
6 x 9, 224 pp, HC, 978-1-59473-039-9 **$21.99**

Creating a Spiritual Retirement: A Guide to the Unseen Possibilities in Our Lives
by Molly Srode 6 x 9, 208 pp, b/w photos, Quality PB, 978-1-59473-050-4 **$14.99**
HC, 978-1-893361-75-1 **$19.95**

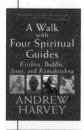

Finding Hope: Cultivating God's Gift of a Hopeful Spirit
by Marcia Ford 8 x 8, 200 pp, Quality PB, 978-1-59473-211-9 **$16.99**

The Geography of Faith: Underground Conversations on Religious, Political and Social
Change *by Daniel Berrigan and Robert Coles* 6 x 9, 224 pp, Quality PB, 978-1-893361-40-9 **$16.95**

Jewish Spirituality: A Brief Introduction for Christians *by Lawrence Kushner*
5½ x 8½, 112 pp, Quality PB, 978-1-58023-150-3 **$12.95** *(a Jewish Lights book)*

Journeys of Simplicity: Traveling Light with Thomas Merton, Bashō, Edward
Abbey, Annie Dillard & Others *by Philip Harnden*
5 x 7¼, 144 pp, Quality PB, 978-1-59473-181-5 **$12.99** 128 pp, HC, 978-1-893361-76-8 **$16.95**

Keeping Spiritual Balance As We Grow Older: More than 65 Creative Ways to
Use Purpose, Prayer, and the Power of Spirit to Build a Meaningful Retirement
by Molly and Bernie Srode 8 x 8, 224 pp, Quality PB, 978-1-59473-042-9 **$16.99**

Spirituality 101: The Indispensable Guide to Keeping—or Finding—Your Spiritual Life
on Campus *by Harriet L. Schwartz, with contributions from college students at nearly thirty campuses across the United States* 6 x 9, 272 pp, Quality PB, 978-1-59473-000-9 **$16.99**

Spiritually Incorrect: Finding God in All the Wrong Places *by Dan Wakefield; Illus. by
Marian DelVecchio* 5½ x 8½, 192 pp, b/w illus., Quality PB, 978-1-59473-137-2 **$15.99**

Spiritual Manifestos: Visions for Renewed Religious Life in America from Young
Spiritual Leaders of Many Faiths *Edited by Niles Elliot Goldstein; Preface by Martin E. Marty*
6 x 9, 256 pp, HC, 978-1-893361-09-6 **$21.95**

A Walk with Four Spiritual Guides: Krishna, Buddha, Jesus, and Ramakrishna
by Andrew Harvey 5½ x 8½, 192 pp, 10 b/w photos & illus., Quality PB, 978-1-59473-138-9 **$15.99**

What Matters: Spiritual Nourishment for Head and Heart
by Frederick Franck 5 x 7¼, 128 pp, 50+ b/w illus., HC, 978-1-59473-013-9 **$16.99**

Who Is My God?, 2nd Edition: An Innovative Guide to Finding Your Spiritual Identity
Created by the Editors at SkyLight Paths 6 x 9, 160 pp, Quality PB, 978-1-59473-014-6 **$15.99**

Spiritual Practice

Soul Fire: Accessing Your Creativity *by Rev. Thomas Ryan, CSP*
Shows you how to cultivate your creative spirit as a way to encourage personal growth.
6 x 9, 160 pp, Quality PB, 978-1-59473-243-0 **$16.99**

Running—The Sacred Art: Preparing to Practice
by Dr. Warren A. Kay; Foreword by Kristin Armstrong
Examines how your daily run can enrich your spiritual life.
5½ x 8½, 160 pp, Quality PB, 978-1-59473-227-0 **$16.99**

Hospitality—The Sacred Art: Discovering the Hidden Spiritual Power
of Invitation and Welcome *by Rev. Nanette Sawyer; Foreword by Rev. Dirk Ficca*
Explores how this ancient spiritual practice can transform your relationships.
5½ x 8½, 192 pp, Quality PB, 978-1-59473-228-7 **$16.99**

Thanking & Blessing—The Sacred Art: Spiritual Vitality through
Gratefulness *by Jay Marshall, PhD; Foreword by Philip Gulley*
Offers practical tips for uncovering the blessed wonder in our lives—even in trying circumstances. 5½ x 8½, 176 pp, Quality PB, 978-1-59473-231-7 **$16.99**

Everyday Herbs in Spiritual Life: A Guide to Many Practices
by Michael J. Caduto; Foreword by Rosemary Gladstar Explores the power of herbs.
7 x 9, 208 pp, 21 b/w illustrations, Quality PB, 978-1-59473-174-7 **$16.99**

Divining the Body: Reclaim the Holiness of Your Physical Self *by Jan Phillips*
8 x 8, 256 pp, Quality PB, 978-1-59473-080-1 **$16.99**

Finding Time for the Timeless: Spirituality in the Workweek
by John McQuiston II Simple stories show you how refocus your daily life.
5½ x 6¾, 208 pp, HC, 978-1-59473-035-1 **$17.99**

The Gospel of Thomas: A Guidebook for Spiritual Practice
by Ron Miller; Translations by Stevan Davies
6 x 9, 160 pp, Quality PB, 978-1-59473-047-4 **$14.99**

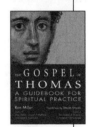

Earth, Water, Fire, and Air: Essential Ways of Connecting to Spirit
by Cait Johnson 6 x 9, 224 pp, HC, 978-1-893361-65-2 **$19.95**

Labyrinths from the Outside In: Walking to Spiritual Insight—A Beginner's Guide
by Donna Schaper and Carole Ann Camp
6 x 9, 208 pp, b/w illus. and photos, Quality PB, 978-1-893361-18-8 **$16.95**

Practicing the Sacred Art of Listening: A Guide to Enrich Your Relationships
and Kindle Your Spiritual Life—The Listening Center Workshop
by Kay Lindahl 8 x 8, 176 pp, Quality PB, 978-1-893361-85-0 **$16.95**

Releasing the Creative Spirit: Unleash the Creativity in Your Life
by Dan Wakefield 7 x 10, 256 pp, Quality PB, 978-1-893361-36-2 **$16.95**

The Sacred Art of Bowing: Preparing to Practice
by Andi Young 5½ x 8½, 128 pp, b/w illus., Quality PB, 978-1-893361-82-9 **$14.95**

The Sacred Art of Chant: Preparing to Practice
by Ana Hernández 5½ x 8¼, 192 pp, Quality PB, 978-1-59473-036-8 **$15.99**

The Sacred Art of Fasting: Preparing to Practice
by Thomas Ryan, CSP 5½ x 8½, 192 pp, Quality PB, 978-1-59473-078-8 **$15.99**

The Sacred Art of Forgiveness: Forgiving Ourselves and Others through God's Grace
by Marcia Ford 8 x 8, 176 pp, Quality PB, 978-1-59473-175-4 **$16.99**

The Sacred Art of Listening: Forty Reflections for Cultivating a Spiritual Practice
by Kay Lindahl; Illustrations by Amy Schnapper
8 x 8, 160 pp, b/w illus., Quality PB, 978-1-893361-44-7 **$16.99**

The Sacred Art of Lovingkindness: Preparing to Practice
by Rabbi Rami Shapiro; Foreword by Marcia Ford 5½ x 8½, 176 pp, Quality PB, 978-1-59473-151-8 **$16.99**

Sacred Speech: A Practical Guide for Keeping Spirit in Your Speech
by Rev. Donna Schaper 6 x 9, 176 pp, Quality PB, 978-1-59473-068-9 **$15.99**
HC, 978-1-893361-74-4 **$21.95**

About SKYLIGHT PATHS Publishing

SkyLight Paths Publishing is creating a place where people of different spiritual traditions come together for challenge and inspiration, a place where we can help each other understand the mystery that lies at the heart of our existence.

Through spirituality, our religious beliefs are increasingly becoming a part of our lives—rather than *apart* from our lives. While many of us may be more interested than ever in spiritual growth, we may be less firmly planted in traditional religion. Yet, we do want to deepen our relationship to the sacred, to learn from our own as well as from other faith traditions, and to practice in new ways.

SkyLight Paths sees both believers and seekers as a community that increasingly transcends traditional boundaries of religion and denomination—people wanting to learn from each other, *walking together, finding the way.*

For your information and convenience, at the back of this book we have provided a list of other SkyLight Paths books you might find interesting and useful. They cover the following subjects:

Buddhism / Zen	Global Spiritual	Monasticism
Catholicism	Perspectives	Mysticism
Children's Books	Gnosticism	Poetry
Christianity	Hinduism /	Prayer
Comparative	Vedanta	Religious Etiquette
Religion	Inspiration	Retirement
Current Events	Islam / Sufism	Spiritual Biography
Earth-Based	Judaism	Spiritual Direction
Spirituality	Kabbalah	Spirituality
Enneagram	Meditation	Women's Interest
	Midrash Fiction	Worship

Or phone, fax, mail or e-mail to: SKYLIGHT PATHS Publishing
Sunset Farm Offices, Route 4 • P.O. Box 237 • Woodstock, Vermont 05091
Tel: (802) 457-4000 • Fax: (802) 457-4004 • www.skylightpaths.com
Credit card orders: (800) 962-4544 (8:30AM–5:30PM ET Monday–Friday)
Generous discounts on quantity orders. SATISFACTION GUARANTEED. Prices subject to change.

For more information about each book,
visit our website at www.skylightpaths.com